Quilt-As-You-Go

QUILT-AS-YOU-GO

Sandra Millett

Chilton Book Company   Radnor, Pennsylvania

All line drawings and photographs by the author

Copyright © 1982 by Sandra Millett
All Rights Reserved
Published in Radnor, Pennsylvania 19089, by Chilton Book Company

Library of Congress Catalog Card No. 81–69052
ISBN 0–8019–7101–2 *hardcover*
ISBN 0–8019–7102–0 *paperback*
Manufactured in the United States of America
Designed by Arlene Putterman

5 6 7 8 9 0   0 9 8 7 6 5 4

This book is dedicated to my husband, Derrill.
His encouragement, interest and help have made my job easier.
And to our children, Pat, Jeff, Pete, Scott and Kathryn,
who have yet to remain silent when stepping on a lost needle!

To the Heritage Quilters of Fresno, who have kept me
pieced together!

Contents

Acknowledgments ix

Introduction 1

One | Quilting Basics 5
QUILTING TERMS, 6   SUPPLIES, 8
MAKING A QUILT-AS-YOU-GO FRAME, 13   STEPS IN MAKING A QUILT, 14

Two | Fabrics: Colors, Kinds, Combinations 17
CHOOSING FABRICS, 18   CHOOSING COLORS, 19
COMBINING PRINTS, 20   PREPARING THE FABRIC, 22

Three | Patterns and Templates 23
CHECKING PATTERN ACCURACY, 24   MAKING TEMPLATES, 25
POSITIONING TEMPLATES, 26   MARKING THE FABRIC, 27
CUTTING AND STORING THE PATCHES, 29

Four | Sample Layouts and Cutting Methods 31
DETERMINING QUILT SIZE, 32   YARDAGE REQUIREMENTS, 33
CUTTING SASHING AND BORDERS, 54   CUTTING BORDER CORNERS, 63

Five | Piecing and Patching 65
JOINING SINGLE EDGES, 66   JOINING MULTIPLE EDGES (FLOPPING), 71
PRESSING, 74   BASTING, 82

Six | Block Assembly 83
METHODS OF ASSEMBLY, 85   SIMPLE APPLIQUE: THE HONEY BEE, 87
SIMPLE MASTER PATTERN, 92

Seven | **Easy, Accurate Applique**   **95**

TRADITIONAL APPLIQUE, 96   MASTER PATTERN APPLIQUE, 97
APPLIQUE RULES, 104
STRAIGHT LINE APPLIQUE: GRANDMOTHER'S FLOWER GARDEN, 105
INTRICATE APPLIQUE: NORTH CAROLINA ROSE, 108   CIRCLES, 119
ELIZABETHAN FLOWER, 122   ADDITIONAL THOUGHTS ON APPLIQUE, 129

Eight | **Piecing and Assembling Difficult Shapes**   **131**

PIECING CURVES, 132   PIECING STARS, 138

Nine | **Strip Assembly**   **155**

MARKING QUILTING PATTERNS, 156   SETTING BLOCKS TO SASHING, 157
CUTTING THE BATT AND BACKING, 157   STRIP ASSEMBLY, 161

Ten | **Quilting As You Go**   **171**

ATTACHING THE STRIP TO THE FRAME, 172   QUILTING, 175
COMPARING THE QUILTING STITCHES, 187

Eleven | **Joining and Binding the Quilt**   **191**

JOINING STRIPS, 192   BINDING THE QUILT, 195   BINDING CORNERS, 203

Twelve | **Drafting Layouts and Figuring Yardage**   **215**

QUILT LAYOUTS, 216   FIGURING YARDAGE, 224

Recommended Reading   **235**

Index   **239**

Acknowledgments

To all my former students, who first asked, "Do you have a book?" and later, "When will it be done?" Their enthusiasm and prodding have kept me motivated.

My thanks and love to Cay Laughton and Marcelle Weigandt, my former partners in the shop, Quilter's Paradise. Their encouragement and understanding in releasing me from our partnership will always be remembered.

To the staff of Boot's Camera, Fresno, California. They have shown great patience in dealing with someone who went from a close-your-eyes-and-hope-for-the-best Instamatic to complicated equipment and, I hope, good photography. Thank you for your understanding, good humor and time.

To my family, to whom this book is dedicated. They have endured less-than-wonderful meals and a messy house with their usual good humor . . . well, most times!

To my eleven-year-old daughter, Kathryn, who did all the posing for the applique close-ups. Thank you for being so patient and interested.

To my friends, who generously loaned the lovely quilts, shown in the color section. Your willingness to share is greatly appreciated.

To Kathryn Conover, my editor, who did such a thoughtful job.

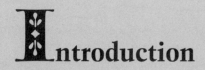

Introduction

It is difficult to imagine that small scraps of fabric, assembled and sewn in a specific or random order, can result in items of exquisite beauty: the result of quilt making. For centuries, quilts have been made for both utilitarian purposes and sheer beauty. Two hundred and fifty years ago small pieces of fabric were cut from worn clothing and simply sewn together to make tops and backs that were then stuffed with corn shucks or dried grass to keep the settlers warm on cold winter nights. Contemporary quilts have become far more sophisticated and, indeed, some are works of art. Making a quilt is not an instant art or something that you you can do overnight. Time, love and tears are sewn into quilts. They are treasures that keep our families warm and are inherited by generations to come.

I am often asked how I started quilting. My mother started me on embroidery when I was seven years of age and knitting when I was nine. These early lessons with a needle led to sewing clothes, doing crewel embroidery and needlepoint, then, logically, to quilting—both as a hobby and a vocation.

While expecting my third child, I decided to make a baby quilt. The basic pattern was taken from a magazine, and I spent three months doing the applique and embroidery work. The directions were easy to follow, until it came to the section on how to quilt. The description was very brief, and though I tried, I just was not satisfied with the results. By then, the birth of my baby was imminent, so the unfinished quilt was put into a drawer and forgotten. While expecting our fourth child, I took the quilt out, removed the hand quilting I was unhappy with and tried to machine quilt. That proved to be even more disastrous, and so the quilt was returned to the drawer. Finally, after our fifth child was born, I took the quilt out again, removed the machine stitching and decided it was time to teach myself to quilt.

I am a self-taught quilter and have experienced the frustration of digging through library after library to find the particular book that answered my question of the moment. And many of the things I read weren't practical. Being a very logical and precise person, I determined that there must be a better, faster and easier way to arrive at the finished product. After reading all the books, I finally decided to learn by doing. I hope that this book will answer the questions I had to struggle with, and that it will save you vast amounts of time and effort.

I have patterned this book after the classes that I teach, and it is intended as a universal guide, both for the beginner and the teacher. However, the experienced quilter should be able to find many new shortcuts.

Prospective students frequently ask if knowledge of sewing is a prerequisite for quilting. My answer is always an emphatic "No!" There are only three simple stitches to master: running stitch, blind stitch and quilting stitch. If 5-year-old girls could be started on piecing and quilting 100 years ago, certainly anyone can learn to master quilt making today. Just remember to learn one step at a time and don't be discouraged by less than perfect results the first time or two. Stick to it and practice; you will improve with each succeeding project.

You will find that I stress accuracy. If a quilt is worth making, it is worth the extra time involved to cut, piece and quilt accurately. Do your best and, again, don't be discouraged.

Quilt-As-You-Go is arranged in the same order in which I teach. Starting with basics, each chapter adds new techniques. I have found that this is the best way for students to learn. Many people assume that they can begin quilting immediately, but piecing must be learned first. Since each new technique is built on a preceding one, it is a good idea to read the book through before you actually begin to work.

Now with scissors and needle at the ready, I wish you happy quilting.

Chapter One

Quilting Basics

If you are new at quilting, it's best to start by learning the basic vocabulary. Below are the words or phrases you will encounter in quilting. You'll find that there may be more than one term for the same definition. In that instance, I will generally use the older, more traditional one. I'll expand on some of the definitions when they are individually discussed in later chapters.

QUILTING TERMS

Quilt: A three-layer bed covering (top, batt and backing) that is held together with a decorative pattern of short stitches going through all three layers. In simple language, it is a fabric sandwich!

Comforter: Similar to a quilt, with a top, batt and backing. The top can be pieced, appliqued or plain, as in a quilt, but it is not joined together with quilting stitches. It is held together with ties through all three layers, placed at regular intervals. Many people use the terms interchangeably, but to tie a unit does not begin to take the time it does to quilt it. Just ask a quilter about a comforter!

Top: The top layer of the quilt. The top may be pieced or appliqued, or it might simply be a large piece of fabric with a quilting design marked on it. In any case, it is the portion you want the world to see.

Batt: The soft middle layer of the quilt. The batt provides the quilt's warmth and fluffiness. Batts may be made from cotton, polyester (my choice) or wool.

Backing or lining: The back, or bottom layer, of the quilt. It can be a solid color or print fabric, and should be similar in weight to the top.

Quilting: The stitching together of the three quilt layers using short, even stitches. The stitches can follow the pattern of the patches or applique, or can follow an elaborate design marked on the top. To have a fine quality quilt, the stitches and the spaces between the stitches should be the same length on the top of the quilt as on the back. That's one of the things that make a quilt of heirloom quality and separate the truly superb quilters from the average!

Patchwork: Joining small pieces of fabrics into a completed design. It can be either pieced or appliqued work.

Block: One finished unit of a quilt pattern. In this book the blocks are 16 inches square.

Piecing: Sewing small pieces of fabric together to form the block, i.e., you piece or applique patchwork.

Applique: Small pieces of fabric arranged in a pattern on a background block and sewn in place with a tiny blind stitch. The finished product is a design of layered fabric.

Setting blocks: Joining finished blocks to form a quilt top. The entire quilt top can be set together into strips for the quilt-as-you-go frame.

Sashing, strips, lattice: Narrow strips of fabric used to separate the blocks. Sashing only goes between blocks, never between a block and border. The sampler quilt must use sashing, because every block is a different pattern and each must be separated from its neighbor so that the individual patterns can be seen.

Border: The fabric strips that surround the completed interior of the quilt, i.e., as a frame surrounds a painting. You can use a single, double or triple border, and multiple borders in some instances. The single border should always be the same color as the sashing. In the case of multiple borders, the inner border and sashing are the same color. This unifies the quilt and helps carry the eye throughout the quilt's design.

Binding: Binding is the narrow finished edge of the quilt. It is sewn over the outside edge of the border to cover the raw edges. It can be either a separate piece of fabric that is sewn on or the backing fabric that has been brought over the edge of the border to the front and sewn down.

Strip, unit: A long section of blocks and sashing, if used, set together and ready to be basted to the batt and backing. The basted strip will go into the quilt-as-you-go frame for quilting.

Marking: Tracing the quilting design onto the quilt top. This can be done before the blocks have been set together and a strip is ready to be basted to the batt and backing. It can also be done after the quilt is in the frame.

Quilt-as-you-go: A method of assembling the quilt top in strips for quilting in a small lap frame. These quilted strips are then joined into a full-size quilt. This method eliminates the need for a large, 10-foot quilting frame and enables you to carry your quilting with you. This technique will be detailed in a later chapter. You do not quilt each block separately since assembly of individual blocks creates major problems.

Quilt patterns: The individual quilt block designs.

Quilting patterns or designs: Patterns for the short quilting stitches. These designs may be very elaborate or just simple straight lines.

Master pattern theory: A method of transferring both applique and quilting designs to the quilt top. This will be discussed in extensive detail in Chapter 7.

Sampler quilt: A quilt in which each block is a different pattern. Sampler quilts use sashing between the blocks so that each block stands alone.

Block-to-block assembly: Each block is the same pattern (usually) and is set together without sashing.

Alternate block assembly: One block is a pieced or appliqued pattern and the next block is plain fabric with a fancy quilting design. The rows are alternated.

SUPPLIES

Most new quilters will find they have many of the quilting supplies on hand. Remember, our early settlers had to make do with very little and usually had only the simplest equipment. If you don't have what I suggest, the key word is *improvise.*

Pencil

Use a soft #2 lead pencil and keep it very sharp! If you tire of constantly sharpening your pencil, buy one that uses separate pieces of lead of *fine* diameter and #B softness. These pencils can be found in stationery, art supply or drafting stores. It is very important to keep in mind that only very light pressure can be used when marking on fabrics. If a line is too dark, it can never be removed. *Never* use a pen on fabric.

Pins

Use fine, sharp pins. I like the ones with glass heads because they are somewhat easier to grip. If you live near a florist, you might want to purchase a box of boutonniere pins. These have long shafts and large heads. In any case, throw away all the old, bent pins you've been using for the last ten years! They're meant to hold the fabric together, not punch holes in it.

Ruler

A short, metal dressmaker's ruler (hemming gauge) works well for making small templates and marking quilting lines. You'll also find that a yardstick will be useful for longer measurements. You might like to try the clear plastic ruler, 18 inches long and 2 inches wide, that is marked off in a grid pattern of $1/16$-inch squares. This can be purchased at either art supply or drafting stores.

Needles

Sharps: These are the long, slender needles with a small eye that are used for all piecing and applique, setting of blocks, sewing strips together and attaching the binding. In short, everything except the quilting will be done with a "sharp." Needles are sized so that the larger the number, the finer the needle. A #8 is larger than a #10, which is the finest "sharp" available for hand sewing. I prefer to use the #10, since it is very fine and glides through the material instead of punching holes. I urge all my students to use it at first, and most find they can handle it quite easily. This needle is so thin that, after a short period of time, it will bend to fit your fingers. This actually makes it easier to use. The only problem comes with threading the tiny eye. One solution is to thread a whole packet of needles onto the spool of thread. When you need more thread, pull it through the eyes of all the needles and leave the last needle on the length cut off. If this needle still presents a problem, try an embroidery needle. They come in the same sizes as "sharps," but the eyes are longer and therefore somewhat easier to thread. In any instance, don't use a needle larger than a #8 unless you have special vision problems.

Quilting or betweens: Quilting needles or betweens (same needle, two names) are used for all the actual quilting. They are short, fat needles with round eyes. I use a #9 needle, which is the finest needle generally available for quilting. If you find this size too difficult to thread, use a #8 or #7. Don't use anything larger than a #7, because it will leave holes in the fabric.

Batts

Polyester batts are made in three ways: bonded, unbonded, and felted or needled. Bonded batts can be bonded on the surface or all through the fibers. Felted batts are quite thin. Both types usually do not shift. Batting sold by the yard is stiff, uneven and really intended for upholstery. Cotton batts shift and need to be quilted every inch, as do unbonded polyester batts.

Thread

There are two types of thread to use. For all piecing and applique and assembly of the quilt, use #50 thread in a color that matches your fabric. This is used with the "sharp" needle. If you are using a variety of colors in the block, choose a thread color that seems to blend well with all the fabrics. You can use cotton-covered polyester or all-cotton thread. I prefer the 100% cotton, since it doesn't twist or get slip knots as readily. All-polyester thread tends to tangle very easily. I wax all my thread to prevent fraying and slipknots.

Quilting thread is so stiff that it should be used only for the actual quilting stitch, not for piecing or applique. It is heavier than #50 thread and is sometimes called "extra-strong" or "super-strength." Do not use buttonhole twist thread, as it is too heavy. Some brands are prewaxed (indicated on the spool). Quilting thread is used only with the quilting or "between" needle.

A white, lightweight thread called Brooks Basting Thread breaks very easily and is meant for temporary stitching or basting. It is much cheaper to use for basting your quilts together than regular mercerized thread.

Beeswax

This was once a common item in a sewing basket, but today only a few women know its purpose. A length of thread is cut from the spool and drawn across the edge or surface of the wax. The wax coats the thread and will greatly decrease the amount of twisting, slipknots and fraying that occurs with hand sewing. If you use polyester thread, you will especially notice the difference. Of course, this applies to all hand sewing, including dressmaking. Remember to remove the excess wax by pulling the thread through your fingers. Beeswax can be purchased in fabric stores or in hardware or sporting goods stores.

Paper

A white paper will be needed for master patterns. You can use white shelf paper, pattern drafting paper, artist's drawing paper or sheets of typewriter paper that have been taped together.

Scissors

It doesn't matter what type you use as long as they are sharp! Keep a separate pair for cutting paper and templates. *Never* use fabric scissors to cut paper.

Template material

This is a sturdy material used to make the actual size patterns. The traditional method for making a template is to draw the pattern as accurately as possible on regular paper and then to cut it out without adding seam allowances. This paper pattern is then glued to the smooth (paper) side of fine sandpaper. (The sandpaper will prevent the template from slipping as you trace around it.) When the glue is dry, the excess sandpaper is cut off at the edge of the pattern. The template is now ready to use. It should be positioned on the wrong side of the fabric (sandpaper side to the fabric) and traced with a pencil. Your pencil line now duplicates the template. Cut the patch from the fabric, adding a ¼-inch seam allowance as you cut.

Many quilters still use the above method, but there are two drawbacks with sandpaper. First, you can't see through the sandpaper, so if you want to center a design, you have to guess at the placement. The second problem is that the edges wear down as you repeatedly trace around them. This makes it impossible to obtain the accuracy necessary when using a pattern like Grandmother's Flower Garden where $\frac{1}{32}$ of an inch can throw off your entire design. The only solution is to replace each template as it begins to wear down. Thus, if you have to cut 3000 hexagons for the quilt top, you'll need to make at least 40 or 50 master templates before you can even put one line on the fabric. That's a lot of extra work!

One way to eliminate these problems is to use a thin, clear, rigid plastic which won't wear away on the edges and has the advantage of transparency for placement of fabric designs. There are several types of plastic that can be used. If you have access to a drafting or art supply store, you can buy acetate Mylar in several thicknesses. I prefer .0075-mil, but either .010- or .005-mil work well also. Be sure to get the type that has a matte or frosty finish on one side. If the Mylar is smooth on both sides you won't be able to write on it. For those quilters who are not able to find Mylar there are several other options. Bacon often comes packaged on plastic sheets that work very nicely and usually have one rough side that can be written on. Some of my students have used old plastic bottles. These are usually not clear and tend to be fairly thick, so care must be used in cutting. Old X-ray film is another source for template material. You can ask hospitals and X-ray labs to save it for you. Rough up one side with fine sandpaper so you'll be able to write on it. Regardless of what template material you use, do not cut it with good fabric scissors; use a pair you don't care about.

Iron

Steam irons work very nicely, but I prefer a plain dry iron used in conjunction with a spray bottle of water. The iron is lighter and its tip is smaller and more pointed than that of a steam iron. Also, my steam iron always burps out big, brown stains just as I place it on the fabric.

MAKING A QUILT-AS-YOU-GO FRAME

The quilt-as-you-go frame is very easy to make. You'll need a hammer, drill, saw and about forty minutes of time. The dowel lengths can be made to fit widths of up to 30 inches or more. All frames will hold a 100-inch strip. For general use, a 24-inch frame (a 48-inch dowel cut in half) is best. I have frames ranging in size from 12 inches to 36 inches, but the latter is really much too long to handle comfortably.

Supplies Needed

1. 24 inches of 1″ × 2″ clear pine or fir. You really can use any type of wood, but if a dense wood such as oak is used, the frame will get a bit heavy to handle.

2. 48 inches of ¾″ dowel or any length desired

3. 4 hanger bolts. These are double-threaded, headless screws (Figure 1–1). They can be purchased separately or in packages that contain swag lamp hooks.

4. 4 #10-24 wing nuts (³⁄₁₆″)

5. 4 #10 flat washers (³⁄₁₆″)

6. 48 inches of 1″-wide canvas tape. The tape has to be light enough to pin into, but not so flimsy that it will stretch. If you can't find it, use pillow ticking or heavy ribbon, such as grosgrain.

7. ⁴⁄₁₆″ upholstery tacks or a staple gun that uses a ¼″ staple leg

8. Epoxy glue or a good white glue

Assembly

1. Cut the 1″ × 2″ pine into two 12″ lengths and sand all the sides smooth.

2. Drill a hole in each end of the 12″ lengths. These holes are to be centered 1″ from each end of the boards. Drill the holes *larger* than the diameter of the

1–1 Use a hanger bolt (shown actual size) for inserting into the drilled dowel holes. They are also called double-threaded screws.

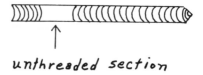

unthreaded section

hanger bolts. (The bolts should be able to slip through easily.) I use a $^7\!/_{32}$" drill bit (Fig. 1–2a).

3. Cut the doweling into two 24" lengths or any length desired. Drill a hole 1" deep into both ends of each length of doweling (Fig. 1–2b). Use a $^3\!/_{16}$" drill bit for this. Be sure that the holes are drilled straight, or the bolts will be at an angle when set in. It helps to have a vise to hold the dowel while you do the drilling.

4. Tack the canvas tape (or whatever you're using) down the length of the doweling, making sure that the tape is in a straight line. Turn ½" of the tape under on each end. Start and end the tape ½" in from the ends of the doweling so that you will have a 23" finished length of tape on the 24" dowel (Fig. 1–2c). If you live in an area of high humidity, coat the tacks or staples with clear nail polish to prevent rust stains on your fabric.

5. Roll the pointed end of the hanger bolt in the prepared glue so that the threads are well covered. Push the bolts into the holes in the ends of the dowel. You may have to tap the bolts lightly with a hammer to coax them in. Be sure you leave the top, threaded area of the bolt sticking out far enough so that you can put the 12" end piece over the bolt and still be able to put on a washer and wing nut (Fig. 1–2d). Let the glue dry thoroughly.

6. Now put the projecting bolts into the end pieces and place a washer and wing nut over the metal portion sticking out of the holes. Notice that in the diagram the dowels have been inserted so that the loose edges of the tape face each other (Fig. 1–2e) and the tacks or staples are on top of the dowels. The arrows indicate which way the dowels are to be rotated after the strip is pinned or basted into the frame.

STEPS IN MAKING A QUILT
When learning any new technique, it's easy to get bogged down in the "how tos" and forget the proper sequence of events. For that reason, I have listed the steps in making a quilt.

1. Choose the pattern.

2. Choose the fabric. These first two steps can be reversed. You might have fabric on hand and look for a block pattern that will enhance it. Or you may fall in love with a particular pattern and then shop for complementary fabrics.

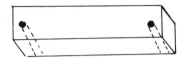

1–2a Drill a hole into each end of the crossbar end.

b Drill centered holes into each end of the dowel.

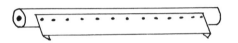

c Attach canvas tape to each dowel, using either upholstery tacks or a staple gun.

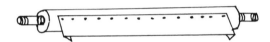

d Roll the long end of the hanger bolt in glue and then tap it into the dowel hole with a hammer.

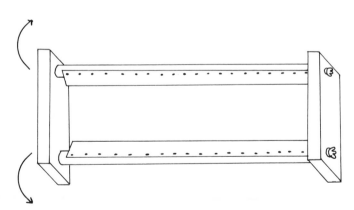

e Insert the projecting bolts into the drilled holes in the end bars.

3. Wash and iron all the fabric. Use hot water to be sure that it has shrunk and bled all its going to. If you're using muslin, wash and dry it at least twice, as it shrinks more than once. The only things you don't wash are the batt and thread.

4. Check your template for accuracy. This is explained in detail in Chapter 3.

5. Cut out the template (see Chapter 3).

6. Use a sharp #2 lead pencil to trace around the template that has been placed on the wrong side of the material (see Chapter 3)

7. Piece or applique the blocks. You must iron as you go when you are piecing. If you are appliqueing, no ironing is necessary, except for the background block. As a general rule, if you piece your entire block and then press it when it's completed, it won't look as crisp as it will if you press each of the small sections as they are completed.

8. Set the blocks together in strips (see Chapter 9).

9. Mark the quilting patterns on the top. For sashing or borders you may choose to do the marking before setting it together (see Chapter 9).

10. Baste the top strip, batt and backing together (see Chapter 9).

11. Set the strip into the quilt-as-you-go frame (see Chapter 10).

12. Quilt the strip (see Chapter 10).

13. Repeat Steps 6 through 12 to make as many strips as necessary for the entire quilt, including the borders. The borders are usually not set to the blocks, but treated as separate strips.

14. Join the strips together to form the interior of the quilt. The quilted border strips are then added to the outer edges of the quilt interior.

15. Bind the edges (see Chapter 11).

16. Enjoy!

One of the terrific things about the quilt-as-you-go method is that once you have two strips made, they can be joined together and you can really see what you are accomplishing. I usually put two strips together and place them across my bed to see how they look. You can even lie down under a long strip to try it out. You may not be covered too completely, but you'll sure look great!

Chapter Two

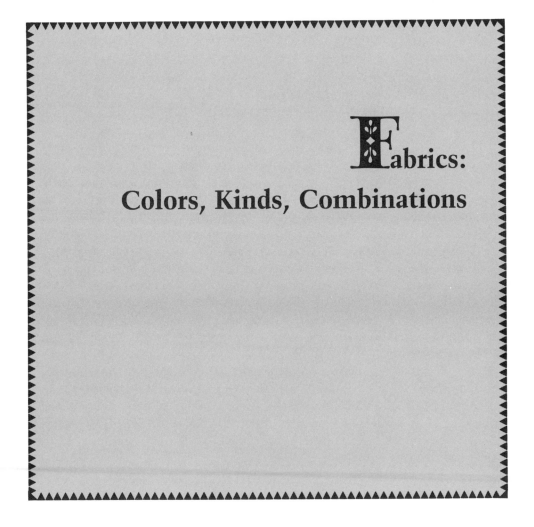

Fabrics:
Colors, Kinds, Combinations

CHOOSING FABRICS

The most important concern of all quilters is what type of fabric to use. Cotton or cotton blend fabrics are generally used for traditional quilts as they are the easiest to work with, especially for a beginner. Also, it has been proven that cotton quilts stand the test of time best. If you can't find 100% cotton, use a cotton blend fabric, but try to avoid 65% polyester, 35% cotton if you are new to quilting. These blends usually fray badly, and a beginner will find it very difficult to handle the small patches. Also, if you are new to my method, where no basting or pressing is done while appliqueing, don't use a high percent blend. If the fabric frays badly or is silky, as is frequently the case with 65/35 blends, you are going to have more problems than necessary.

Try to choose fabrics that have a good, tight weave. If you are a beginner, try to use as much 100% cotton or 50/50 blend as possible. If you can't find the color or print you need in these blends, you'll have no choice but to use a 65/35 fabric. A number of quilters are hesitant to use cotton because of its tendency to wrinkle and bleed. Remember, cotton fabrics today are not what they were twenty or thirty years ago. Many are permanent press and need little or no ironing. The modern fabrics don't usually bleed color as they used to either, but always wash your fabric to shrink it and remove any excess dye and finish.

It doesn't matter if you use scraps on hand or buy all new fabric, as long as the materials are all similar in weight and fiber content. Do not use seer-sucker (too puckery), sheer fabrics, laces, or single or double knits. While knits work well for simple shapes, i.e., squares, triangles and rectangles that are machine pieced, they are usually too thick for involved hand piecing or applique, and they make very heavy seams. However, if you want to try them, I wish you luck!

Polyester has been so popular during the last ten years that you may not have many cotton scraps on hand. If you do have scraps you want to use, you're ahead of the game. In that case, you will probably need to purchase only the fabric for sashing, borders and backing. If you don't have scraps, all the fabric will have to be purchased. In either case, the colors should be coordinated to tie the quilt together visually (see color Fig. 3).

CHOOSING COLORS

Probably the biggest problem for new quilters is choosing colors. After selecting material for a few quilts, you'll find it will be one of the most exciting tasks in making a quilt. At first you may feel completely lost, but there are some guides to follow and it really does get easier.

The best single item to help you is a color wheel, commonly used by artists and decorators. It is a circle that is divided equally into 12 solid color wedges, starting with yellow at the top and moving in color succession as a rainbow. Although we quilters work with fabrics that can have many colors in their designs, usually a fabric has a dominant color (it may not be the background color), and that would be the color on the wheel. It would help a great deal for you to make a color wheel from patterned fabrics, as shown in color Fig. 12. Take it with you when shopping to help in selecting colors. I have provided a color wheel template so that you can make your own (Fig. 2–1).

Using a color wheel is not difficult. There are a number of methods in working from the wheel. Select from one of the groupings listed below, stick to it and your quilt will be very eye-catching.

Triad: Three colors that are an equal distance apart on the wheel; in other words, every fourth color. Let's suppose you want to use orange. Green and purple are the triads. You may not care for the strong, pure colors, but what if you use the softer tones of peach, pale green and lavender? Yellow, blue and red softened with white are pale yellow, baby blue and pink. Now you know why those three colors look so good in a baby's room; it's a triad. You could also use one strong color, blue-violet (blueberry), light grass green (lime) and soft red-orange (light rust).

Complementary: Opposite colors on the wheel complement each other. Green and red (Christmas) or purple and yellow are examples.

Analogous: Colors that are next to each other on the color wheel. The cool colors are the greens, blues and purples. The warm colors are reds, oranges and yellows.

Polychromatic: This is a color scheme using all of the colors from around the color wheel: yellow, green, blue, purple, red and orange.

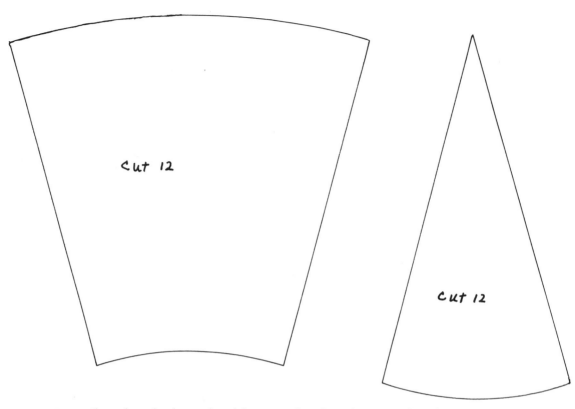

2–1 The color wheel template (also see color Fig. 12). Cut twelve of each patch. Piece the wheel following the directions in Chapter 8.

Achromatic: These are the neutral colors: white, black, brown, beige and gray. These colors are not found on the color wheel, because they are really "noncolors."

Monochromatic: A one-color scheme. For example, the palest pink, bright pink, red and deep, ruby red.

COMBINING PRINTS

Harmonious (pleasing) colors play a very important part in the overall effect of your quilt; but equally important is the mixture of solid colors and prints. Strong solid colors in a geometric pattern will look very contemporary. A mixture of small prints in faded colors will have an old, very traditional feel. The combination of solids, prints and colors are endless, and selecting them

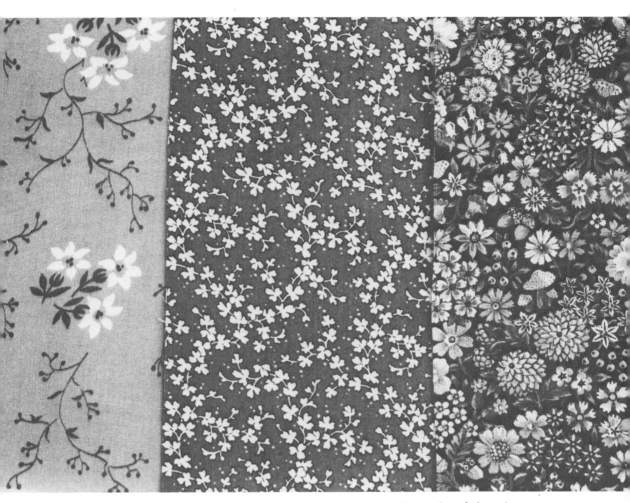

2–2 **Examples of the print mixing formula. In a black-and-white photo the designs and background variations become very pronounced.**

offers you a challenging job, for you will want your quilt to "fit" the location you have chosen for it.

For years, while growing up, you were told that you couldn't wear two prints at the same time and, if you tried three, Heaven forbid, the world would surely end! As a quilter you must forget those early lessons. Two or more prints do go together, and more often than not, they add more interest than just a variety of solid colors and one print.

The burning question is, how do you choose not only the right colors, but compatible prints? I pick one fabric I like, either a print or solid, then try different color and print combinations until I'm satisfied. Sometimes, by my final selection, I have eliminated the original fabric choice. Remember, be flexible! Don't feel you must use a fabric just because you happen to have it. You'll eventually find the right spot for it in another quilt.

It can take from ten minutes in one store, to days in many stores, to find that final "perfect" piece of fabric. When I was a partner in a quilt shop, I had one customer who came in two days in a row and spent four hours each day selecting fabric for a quilt. I was numb by then, and she had wasted seven hours. Sometimes your first instincts are the best. Too much pondering leads to confusion!

My formula for mixing prints pleasingly was acquired while helping many customers select the right combination. I found that when working in conjunction with the color wheel, you can effectively mix fabrics with the following design combinations: (Fig. 2–2).

1. A print with lots of background color showing and little pattern design;
2. An even mixture of background color and pattern design;
3. Heavy pattern design, with little background color showing.

If you use this print formula, along with the color wheel, you'll find fabric selection much easier and really a lot of fun.

PREPARING THE FABRIC

Some fabrics will shrink more than others. You need to eliminate all shrinkage before you start piecing. Wash all fabrics in hot water and dry them on your dryer's "hot" setting. Wash and dry muslin twice. After the fabric is washed, iron it, if necessary. *Do not* wash the batt or thread.

Chapter Three

atterns and Templates

CHECKING PATTERN ACCURACY

While you are preparing the fabric, the templates can be made. How do you know if the block pattern a friend has given you, or that you found in a book, is accurate? You don't; therefore, you *must* assume that it is inaccurate. I know that this is a blow to most of you, especially those of you who have a large library of quilting books. If your pieced blocks haven't been lying flat when completed, this is the reason. Of all the books I own, there are only two or maybe three with which I feel safe working directly from the patterns. I don't let this stop me from purchasing books, however. I use them as resource material and as a starting point for drafting.

Certainly your next question must be, "Why the inaccuracy?" There are several reasons. A number of the old books are reprints from newspapers, and the distortion from the printing presses has been magnified over the years. In the newer books, again some distortion has occurred because of the printing, but it can't all be blamed on the reproduction process. Some authors and publishing houses do not realize how critical accuracy in quilt patterns is.

I think most of us believe that all "old time" quilts were perfect. If you take a really close look (or many times just a glance), you'll find that this is not the case. There were women then, as now, who didn't enjoy quilting, but had no choice in the matter. Bed coverings had to be made! Of the thousands of quilts that have been made, worn out and discarded, many were just "thrown together." When I see a quilt like that, I feel a particular kinship with the maker. One hundred years ago that woman had to do things she wasn't very crazy about either, but she had no alternatives.

How can you tell if your pattern is accurate? First, simply look at it. Some patterns are so far off you can see that template A is too long to fit to template B. The next step is to measure each of the template edges. If it's a square, all the sides should be the same length and have right-angle corners (90 degrees). Check each of the patch patterns with a ruler to see if the edges that will be sewn together are the same length. If not, then something is going to have to be done about it. Sometimes it's as simple as moving one line just a bit, but more often than not, it means that you will have to work with graph paper and a ruler. Please, don't let that scare you away; it is not as hard as you might think. Drafting patterns is covered in detail in Chapter 12.

MAKING TEMPLATES

After making sure that your pattern is accurate, you must make a template for each of the patches. It is extremely important that all marking and cutting be done carefully.

Note: For hand piecing, seam allowances *should not* be added to the template patterns. They will be allowed for when cutting. If you are making templates for machine piecing, then you *must* add a ¼-inch seam allowance to the template.

Place the template material (assuming you are using clear, Mylar plastic) over the accurate paper pattern. Using a ruler as a guide, trace over the pattern line to duplicate the pattern on the plastic. Be sure that you have made an exact copy, paying special attention to the corners. Use an old, but sharp, pair of scissors to cut out the template. Be accurate in cutting, and make sure the points are nice and sharp with straight edges. Now lay the plastic template back over the original pattern to check it for accuracy. If the template doesn't match the pattern, don't use it; make a better one. Be sure not to cut out the original paper pattern as a template. Keep it as a permanent reference.

If you are not using plastic, then use a piece of typing or writing paper and position it over the accurate pattern. With a ruler as a guide, copy the template pattern onto the typing paper. If you have trouble seeing the lines of the pattern through the typing paper, tape both pieces of paper to a window and the lines will be visible. Cut out the template copy and glue it to a firm piece of opaque plastic (coffee can lid) or stiff paper, such as a manila folder. The paper side of fine sandpaper can also be used. Let the glue dry and then cut the excess stiff template material away. Do remember, if you use a cardboard or sandpaper template, it will wear down after repeated use and, you'll need to make others (see Chapter 1).

I have mentioned accuracy quite a few times. I know that at this point it probably sounds picky to you to make such a fuss about it, but a little extra care now will save you much agony later on. I have seen finished blocks, for the same quilt, that varied as much as three inches in size; a Lone Star that rippled like a wave and would never lie flat; a Broken Star so large it flowed twelve inches onto the floor.

POSITIONING TEMPLATES

You are almost ready to mark and cut the fabric, but you must be aware of fabric straight-of-grain before placing your template on the material.

Cotton fabric is made by first stringing threads lengthwise on a loom; then another thread is interwoven through each of the lengthwise threads. The threads running the length of the fabric are called the "warp" and the threads interweaving them are the "woof." The woven edge of the fabric is called the "selvage." The selvages frequently shrink a great deal when washed and, thus, should be cut off and discarded. The actual straight-of-grain is the warp, but for a quilter both the warp and woof can be considered the straight. If you pull on the diagonal, there will be a great deal of give. This is the "bias." A true bias is on a 45-degree angle to the selvage.

When you trace the template on fabric, you should have as many straight edges of the template on the straight-of-grain as possible. The following dia-

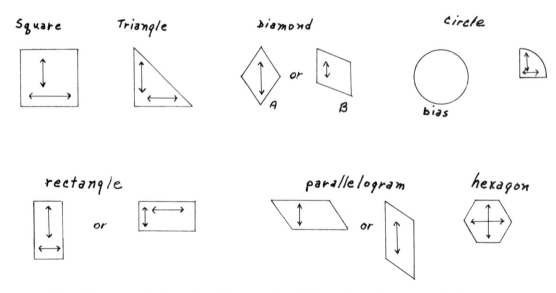

3–1   The arrows indicate the directions in which to place the geometric shapes on fabric straight-of-grain.

grams have arrows indicating the direction in which the templates should be placed on the fabric (Fig. 3–1). Both the warp and woof are given for the square and triangle. I have given two choices for the diamond. In diamond A, the straight is placed down the center length of the diamond and all the edges are on the bias. Cutting diamond B places two edges on the straight and two on the bias. Diamonds are frequently used to make stars where the most tension would be from point to point; therefore diamond A would be used most often. The same applies to the parallelogram, in that two placements are possible. The hexagon can have only two edges on the grain because of its shape. A circle, of course, has no straight sides, so all the edges are on the bias.

Now that I've given you some rules to follow, I'm going to contradict myself and say that you can disregard them if you want to. If there is a pattern or stripe in the fabric that you want to take advantage of, the template can be placed accordingly. This will frequently be the case with odd-shaped applique patches, where most of the edges are on the bias. If possible, try to have the straight running the longest span of the template. You must be very careful in sewing and pressing these patches, since all bias edges will stretch very easily.

MARKING THE FABRIC

Your fabric should now be prepared: washed, dried and ironed. Lay it on a table, wrong side up. Place the template, matte or sandpaper side down, on the fabric following the straight-of-grain or fabric design and close enough to the edge to leave a ¼-inch seam allowance around it if you are hand piecing.

Using a very sharp #2 pencil (no pens, please), mark around the edge of the template so that the template outline is duplicated on the fabric with a fine, light line. The fabric will tend to shift and pull, especially at the template corners. If you hold the pencil at an angle and draw it across the fabric, the pulling is not quite as bad. Working with a sharp pencil and lifting it occasionally to let the fabric return to its normal position helps too. Press down just hard enough to mark the fabric; you don't need a heavy, dark line. Try to train yourself to draw only a *single* line. Avoid scratching around the template. A single, fine line will do.

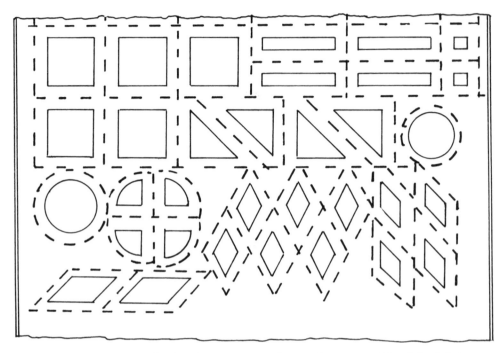

3–2 **Various templates for hand piecing traced onto the wrong side of the fabric. A ½-inch space is left between each shape to allow for seam allowances. The cutting lines are indicated by broken lines.**

On some print or dark fabrics, pencil lines won't show. For these materials use a sliver of white soap for the marking instead of a pencil. After your hand soap has been used down to a small piece, let it dry on a windowsill for a few days; the edge will make a good marker. Don't use colored soap, since the dye might leave a stain on the fabric. The soap-marked patches need to be handled carefully, since the soap lines will rub off. A tailor's chalk pencil can be used instead, but I have found that they don't sharpen well. Also you have to apply a lot of pressure to make a line. There is a water soluble pen available today that is terrific; however, some types tend to vanish in a few days.

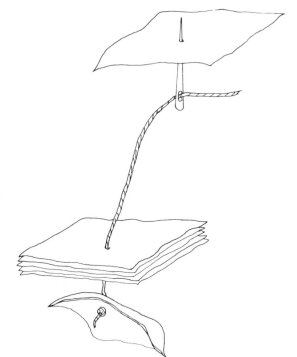

3–3 String all the patches of one shape onto a knotted thread.

CUTTING AND STORING THE PATCHES

For hand piecing, the template lines have been drawn on the fabric so that there is a ¼-inch space around each shape. In other words, there is ½-inch between each of the shapes. Using sharp scissors, cut down the middle of the space between the patches; this will automatically leave a ¼-inch seam allowance on each patch (Fig. 3–2).

In this book I deal only with hand work, both for piecing and quilting, but the techniques are basically the same for machine work. When machine piecing, the templates have the seam allowances included, so the pencil lines become the cutting lines. With most sewing machines, the distance from the outer edge of the presser foot to the needle is ¼ inch. Check your machine to see if there is a variation and then make the necessary adjustments when sewing. The patches are fed into the machine with the cut edges lined up with the presser foot edge. The stitching line will automatically leave a ¼-inch seam allowance.

After the patches have been cut they tend to get lost if not contained in some way. Boxes filled with neat stacks of patches are always being knocked over, and then confusion reigns. It's a good idea to string each pile of matching patches onto a knotted, white thread (Fig. 3–3). The knot is placed at the bottom of the stack and a patch is pulled off the loose thread as needed. It's difficult to tell some patches apart, so make a label from scrap fabric and mark it with the patch designation. String the label onto the knotted thread first, so it will be on the bottom of the stack.

Chapter Four

Sample Layouts
and Cutting Methods

DETERMINING QUILT SIZE

How do you determine the quantity of fabric for a quilt project? Basically, a double-size quilt top with a 12-inch drop uses 6 yards and a king to the floor uses 12 to 17 yards, depending on the size of the patches. More and smaller patches mean many more seam allowances, and those $\frac{1}{4}$-inch allowances really gobble up the yardage.

Let's assume you want to make a double-bed quilt in three colors. If the three colors are going to be used in equal amounts, divide the 6 yards needed by the three colors. You'll need 2 yards of each color. I would buy $2\frac{1}{2}$ yards of each to allow for shrinkage and mistakes.

Because this book deals with a sampler quilt, made to specific sizes, yardages have to be more than a "guesstimate." First, determine what size quilt is needed. Only then can you figure the yardage amounts accurately. (See Chapter 12 for detailed instructions on figuring yardage.) If you are trying to fit a particular bed, you must measure it to determine how large the quilt needs to be. Start with the mattress dimensions below.

Mattress Top Measurements (in inches):

Crib	28 × 52
Twin	38 × 75
Double	54 × 75
Queen	60 × 75
King	72 × 85
Waterbed	72 × 104 to 108

There are many additional factors that must be taken into account in determining quilt size. Do you want the quilt to be used with a skirt? Mattress thickness varies, with foam at 5 inches to innerspring ranging from 5 to 7 inches. If the quilt is to hang to the floor, is your bed on regular legs or casters? Large casters add 2 inches to the distance from mattress edge to floor. If you want the quilt to just touch the floor, as a bedspread would, that's important. How thick are the pillows? Big, fat ones need more quilt to cover them. If you intend to tuck the quilt under the pillows, it will add another 4 to 5 inches to the length. Maybe none of the above seems important to you; all you want to do is just make a quilt! That's fine too. Pick out the size that you want and get to work. But if you are going to make a quilt for a specific bed, then overall finished measurements are vital.

The actual quilting stitch draws up the quilt and reduces the finished size. Depending on how elaborate your quilting pattern is, you may have to add an extra 2 inches to both the length and width. These 2 inches should go into the borders, where your final size adjustments will be made. One of the advantages of quilt-as-you-go is that you can finish the entire interior of the quilt and lay it on the bed for a "fitting." Then you can tell if you need more or less width in the borders and, when finished, the quilt edge will be exactly where you want it.

The normal drop for a quilt used with a skirt is the mattress measurement plus 12 inches for each of the sides and bottom and 9 to 12 inches for a pillow allowance. For a quilt that drops to the floor, you would add 18 to 21 inches. For example, a double-bed mattress measures 54 by 75 inches. To make a quilt that will be used with a skirt, add 12 inches for each side to the 54-inch mattress width to get 78 inches. The 75-inch length is added to a 12-inch drop for the foot and a 9-inch fold-over for the pillow, for a total of 96 inches. Your quilt will measure 78 by 96 inches.

Below, I list some basic sizes for quilts intended to be used with a skirt or to extend to the floor. These are average sizes; your own needs may vary with your bed measurements.

Finished Quilt Sizes (in inches):

Bed Type	With Skirt (12-inch drop)	To the Floor
Throw or Crib	44 × 64	—
Twin	62 × 96	78 × 104
Double	78 × 96	94 × 104
Queen	84 × 96	100 × 104
King	96 × 106	112 × 114
King Waterbed	80 × 117 (4-inch tuck)	

YARDAGE REQUIREMENTS

Sampler quilts must have sashing or alternate blocks to separate the different block patterns. In Figures 4–1 through 4–20 you are given ten quilt

Text continues on page 54

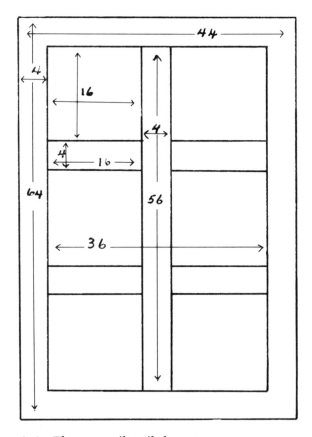

4–1 Throw or crib quilt layout.

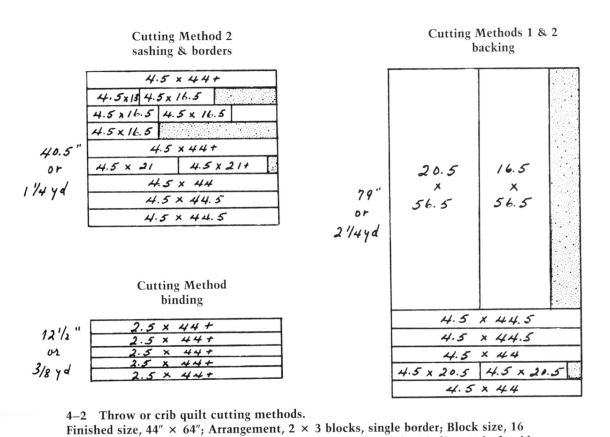

Cutting Method 2
sashing & borders

4.5 × 44+		
4.5×13	4.5 × 16.5	
4.5 × 16.5	4.5 × 16.5	
4.5 × 16.5		
4.5 × 44+		
4.5 × 21	4.5 × 21+	
4.5 × 44		
4.5 × 44.5		
4.5 × 44.5		

40.5"
or
1 1/4 yd

Cutting Method
binding

| 2.5 × 44+ |
| 2.5 × 44+ |
| 2.5 × 44+ |
| 2.5 × 44+ |
| 2.5 × 44+ |

12 1/2 "
or
3/8 yd

Cutting Methods 1 & 2
backing

| 20.5 × 56.5 | 16.5 × 56.5 | |

79"
or
2 1/4 yd

4.5 × 44.5	
4.5 × 44.5	
4.5 × 44	
4.5 × 20.5	4.5 × 20.5
4.5 × 44	

4–2 Throw or crib quilt cutting methods.
Finished size, 44″ × 64″; Arrangement, 2 × 3 blocks, single border; Block size, 16 inches square; Sashing, 4 inches wide; Borders, 4 inches wide; Binding, ½ inch wide. Yardage required: Sashing & borders, 1¼ yards; Backing, 2¼ yards; Binding, ⅜ yard.

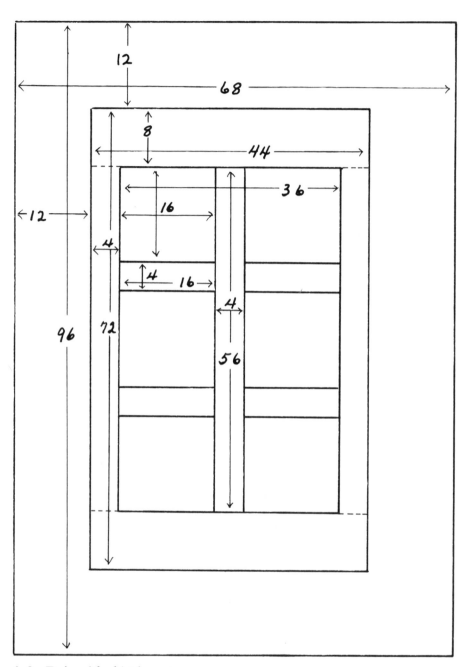

4–3 Twin with skirt layout.

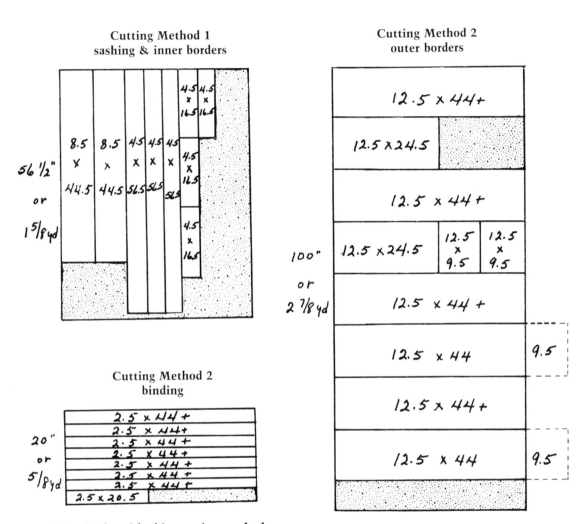

Cutting Method 1
sashing & inner borders

56 1/2"
or
1 5/8 yd

4.5 x 16.5 4.5 x 16.5
8.5 x 44.5 8.5 x 44.5 4.5 x 56.5 4.5 x 56.5 4.5 x 56.5 4.5 x 16.5
4.5 x 16.5

Cutting Method 2
outer borders

100"
or
2 7/8 yd

12.5 x 44+
12.5 x 24.5
12.5 x 44+
12.5 x 24.5   12.5 x 9.5   12.5 x 9.5
12.5 x 44+
12.5 x 44   9.5
12.5 x 44+
12.5 x 44   9.5

Cutting Method 2
binding

20"
or
5/8 yd

2.5 x 44+
2.5 x 44+
2.5 x 44+
2.5 x 44+
2.5 x 44+
2.5 x 44+
2.5 x 20.5

4–4 Twin with skirt cutting methods.
Finished size, 68″ × 96″; Arrangement, 2 × 3 blocks, double border; Block size, 16 inches square; Sashing, 4 inches wide; Inner border, 4 inches wide (sides), 8 inches wide (top & bottom); Outer border, 12 inches wide; Binding, ½ inch wide.
Yardage required: Sashing & inner border, 1⅝ yards; Outer borders, 2⅞ yards; Backing, 5½ yards; Binding, ⅝ yard.

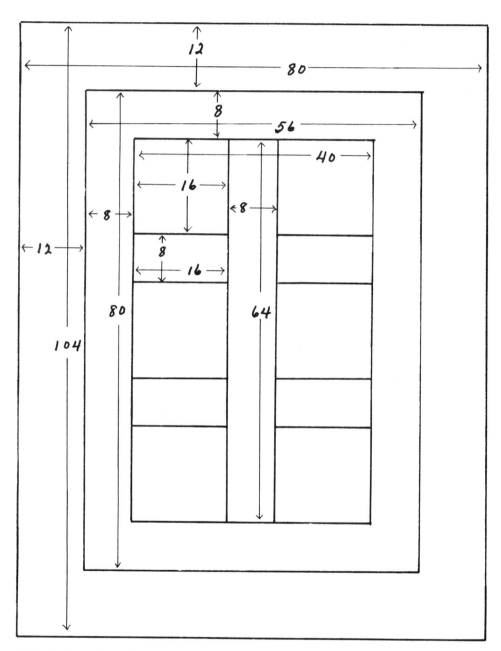

4–5 Twin to floor layout.

Cutting Method 1
sashing & inner border

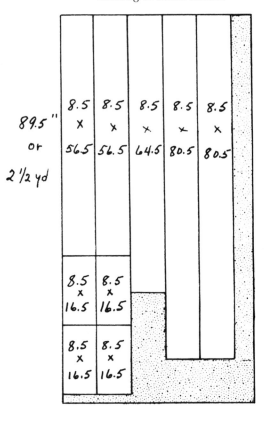

89.5"
or
2½ yd

| 8.5 × 56.5 | 8.5 × 56.5 | 8.5 × 64.5 | 8.5 × 80.5 | 8.5 × 80.5 |

8.5 × 16.5 | 8.5 × 16.5

8.5 × 16.5 | 8.5 × 16.5

Cutting Method 2
outer border

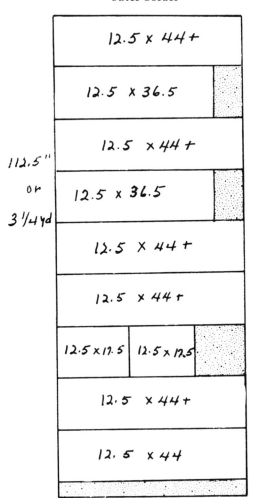

112.5"
or
3¼ yd

12.5 × 44+
12.5 × 36.5
12.5 × 44+
12.5 × 36.5
12.5 × 44+
12.5 × 44+
12.5 × 17.5 | 12.5 × 12.5
12.5 × 44+
12.5 × 44

Cutting Method 2
binding

22.5"
or
5/8 yd

2.5 × 44+
2.5 × 44+
2.5 × 44+
2.5 × 44+
2.5 × 44+
2.5 × 44+
2.5 × 44+
2.5 × 44+
2.5 × 21.5

4–6   Twin to floor cutting methods.
Finished size, 80″ × 104″; Arrangement, 2 × 3 blocks, double borders; Block size, 16 inches square; Sashing, 8 inches wide; Inner borders, 8 inches wide; Outer borders, 12 inches wide; Binding, ½ inch wide.
Yardage required: Sashing & inner borders, 2½ yards; Outer borders, 3¼ yards; Backing, 5½ yards; Binding, 5/8 yard.

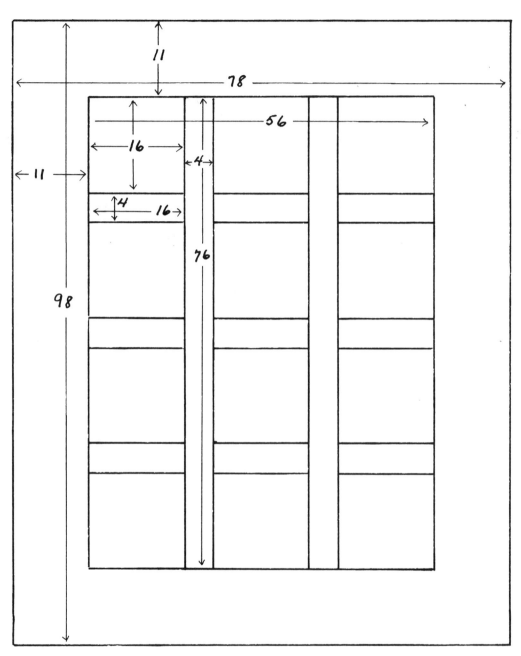

4-7 Double with skirt layout.

Cutting Method 1

138"

or

3 7/8 yd

11.5 X 98.5

11.5 X 98.5

11.5 X 78.5

4.5 X 76.5

4.5 X 76.5

4.5 X 16.5

4.5 X 16.5

4.5 X 16.5

4.5 X 16.5

4.5 X 16.5

4.5 X 16.5

4.5 X 16.5

11.5 X 39.5

11.5 X 39.5

4.5 X 16.5

4.5 X 16.5

4.5 X 16.5

4.5 X 16.5

Join

Cutting Method 2

22.5"

or

7/8 yd

2.5 × 44 +
2.5 × 44 +
2.5 × 44 +
2.5 × 44 +
2.5 × 44 +
2.5 × 44 +
2.5 × 44 +
2.5 × 44

2.5 × 5

4–8 Double with skirt cutting methods.
Finished size, 78" × 98"; Arrangement, 3 × 4 blocks, single border; Block size, 16 inches square; Sashing, 4 inches wide; Borders, 11 inches wide; Binding, ½ inch wide.
Yardage required: Sashing & borders, 3⅞ yards; Backing, 6 yards; Binding, ⅞ yard.

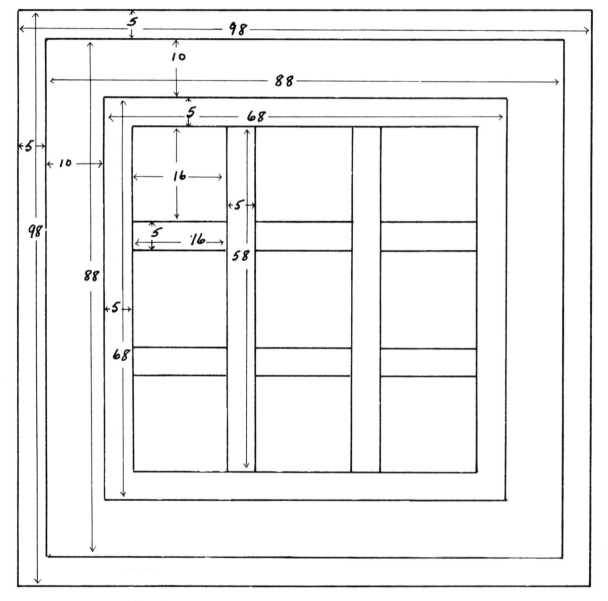

4–9 Double to floor layout.

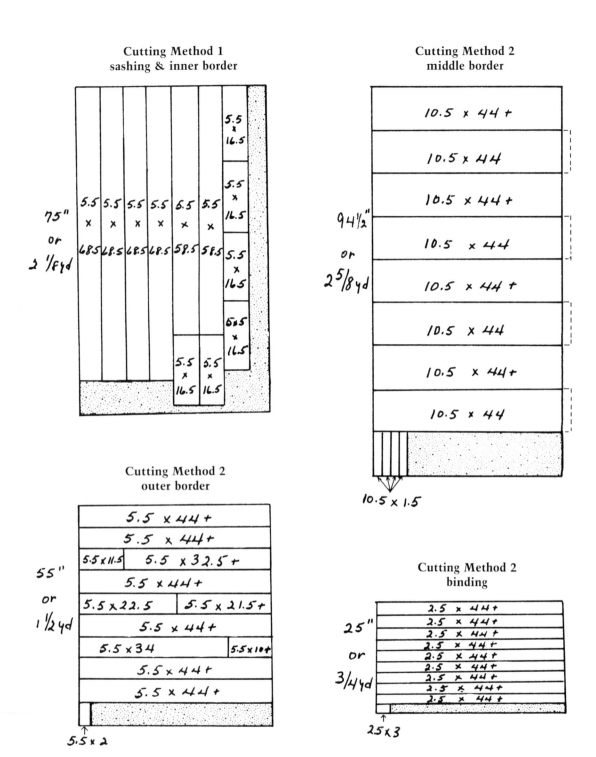

Cutting Method 1
sashing & inner border

75"
or
2 1/8 yd

5.5 x 16.5

5.5 x 16.5

5.5 x 16.5

5.5 x 16.5

5.5 x 16.5

5.5 | 5.5 | 5.5 | 5.5 | 6.5 | 5.5
x | x | x | x | x | x
68.5 | 68.5 | 68.5 | 68.5 | 58.5 | 58.5

5.5 x 16.5 | 5.5 x 16.5

Cutting Method 2
middle border

94½"
or
2 5/8 yd

10.5 x 44 +
10.5 x 44
10.5 x 44 +
10.5 x 44
10.5 x 44 +
10.5 x 44
10.5 x 44 +
10.5 x 44

10.5 x 1.5

Cutting Method 2
outer border

55"
or
1 ½ yd

5.5 x 44 +
5.5 x 44 +
5.5 x 11.5 | 5.5 x 32.5 +
5.5 x 44 +
5.5 x 22.5 | 5.5 x 21.5 +
5.5 x 44 +
5.5 x 34 | 5.5 x 10 +
5.5 x 44 +
5.5 x 44 +

5.5 x 2

Cutting Method 2
binding

25"
or
3/4 yd

2.5 x 44 +
2.5 x 44 +
2.5 x 44 +
2.5 x 44 +
2.5 x 44 +
2.5 x 44 +
2.5 x 44 +
2.5 x 44 +
2.5 x 44 +

2.5 x 3

4–10 Double to floor cutting methods.
Finished size, 98″ × 98″; Arrangement, 3 × 3 blocks, triple borders; Block size, 16 inches square; Sashing, 5 inches wide; Inner borders, 5 inches wide; Middle borders, 10 inches wide; Outer borders, 5 inches wide; Binding, ½ inch wide.
Yardage required: Sashing & inner borders, 2⅛ yards; Middle borders, 2⅝ yards; Outer borders, 1½ yards; Backing, 7½ yards; Binding, ¾ yard.

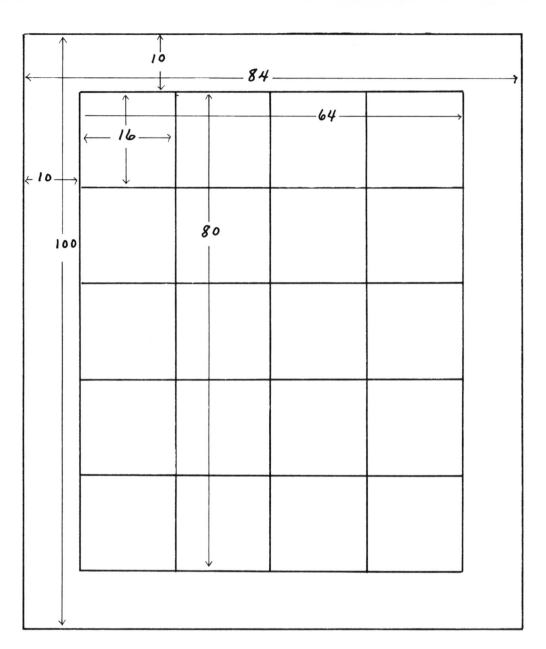

 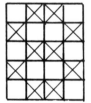

Two possible alternate
block arrangements

4–11   Queen with skirt layout.

Cutting Method 1
alternate blocks

16.5 x 16.5	16.5 x 16.5	
16.5 x 16.5	16.5 x 16.5	
16.5 x 16.5	16.5 x 16.5	
16.5 x 16.5	16.5 x 16.5	
16.5 x 16.5	16.5 x 16.5	

82½"
or
2⅜ yd

Cutting Method 2
border

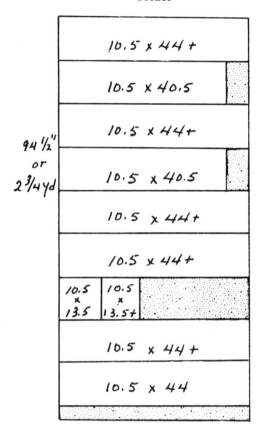

10.5 x 44 +
10.5 x 40.5
10.5 x 44 +
10.5 x 40.5
10.5 x 44 +
10.5 x 44 +
10.5 x 13.5 | 10.5 x 13.5 +
10.5 x 44 +
10.5 x 44

94½"
or
2¾ yd

Cutting Method 2
binding

2.5 x 44 +
2.5 x 44 +
2.5 x 44 +
2.5 x 44 +
2.5 x 44 +
2.5 x 44 +
2.5 x 44 +
2.5 x 44 +
2.5 x 22.5

22½"
or
⅞ yd

4–12 Queen with skirt cutting methods.
Finished size, 84″ × 100″; Arrangement, 4 × 5 alternate blocks, single border; Block size, 16 inches square; Borders, 10 inches wide; Binding, ½ inch wide.
Yardage required: Alternate blocks, 2⅜ yards; Borders, 2¾ yards; Backing, 7⅜ yards; Binding, ⅞ yard.

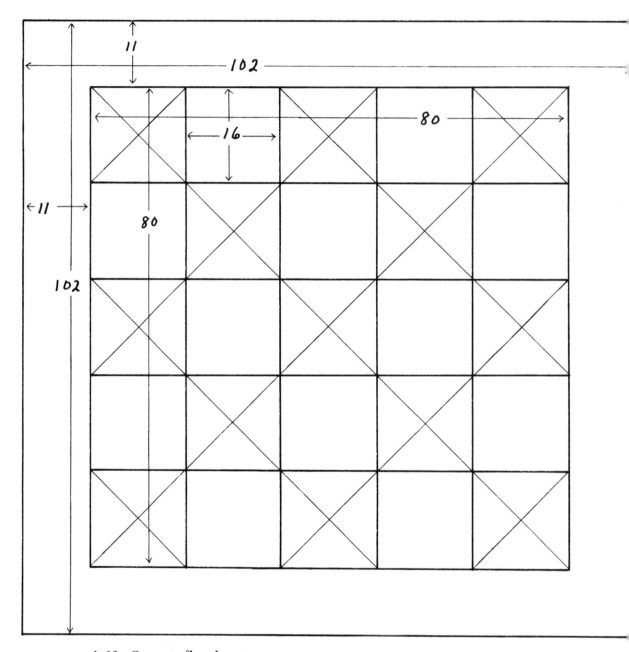

4–13 Queen to floor layout.

Cutting Method 1
alternate blocks

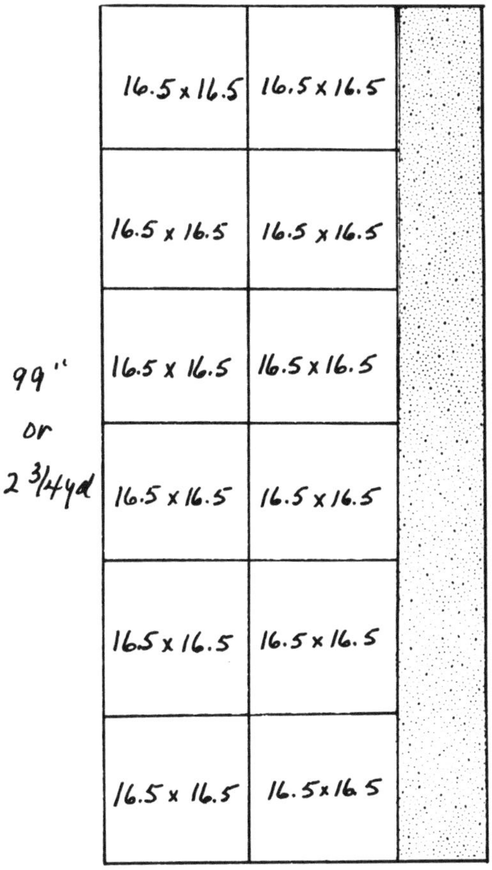

16.5 x 16.5	16.5 x 16.5	
16.5 x 16.5	16.5 x 16.5	
16.5 x 16.5	16.5 x 16.5	
16.5 x 16.5	16.5 x 16.5	
16.5 x 16.5	16.5 x 16.5	
16.5 x 16.5	16.5 x 16.5	

99"
or
2 3/4 yd

Cutting Method 2
border

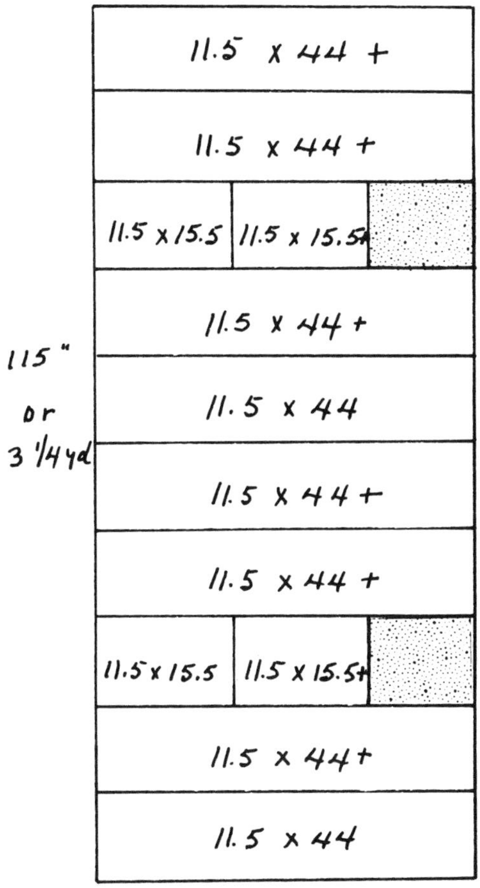

115"
or
3 1/4 yd

11.5 x 44 +		
11.5 x 44 +		
11.5 x 15.5	11.5 x 15.5+	
11.5 x 44 +		
11.5 x 44		
11.5 x 44 +		
11.5 x 44 +		
11.5 x 15.5	11.5 x 15.5+	
11.5 x 44+		
11.5 x 44		

Cutting Method 2
binding

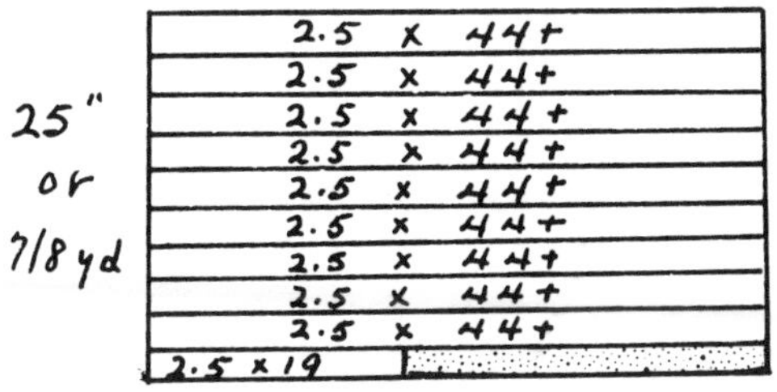

25"
or
7/8 yd

2.5 x 44+
2.5 x 44+
2.5 x 44 +
2.5 x 44 +
2.5 x 44 +
2.5 x 44 +
2.5 x 44 +
2.5 x 44 +
2.5 x 44 +
2.5 x 19

4–14 Queen to floor cutting methods.
Finished size, 102″ × 102″; Arrangement, 5 × 5 alternate blocks, single border;
Block size, 16 inches square; Borders, 11 inches wide; Binding, ½ inch wide.
Yardage required: Alternate blocks, 2¾ yards; Borders, 3¼ yards; Backing, 7½ yards;
Binding, ⅞ yard.

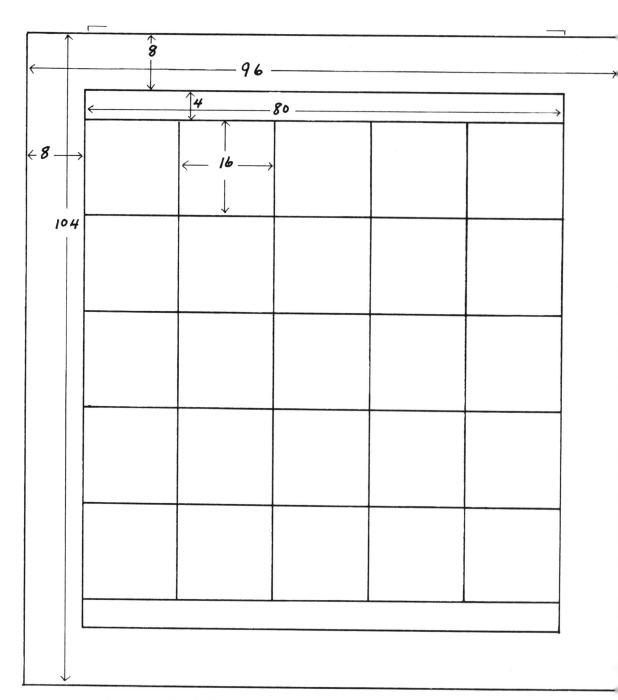

4–15   King with skirt layout.

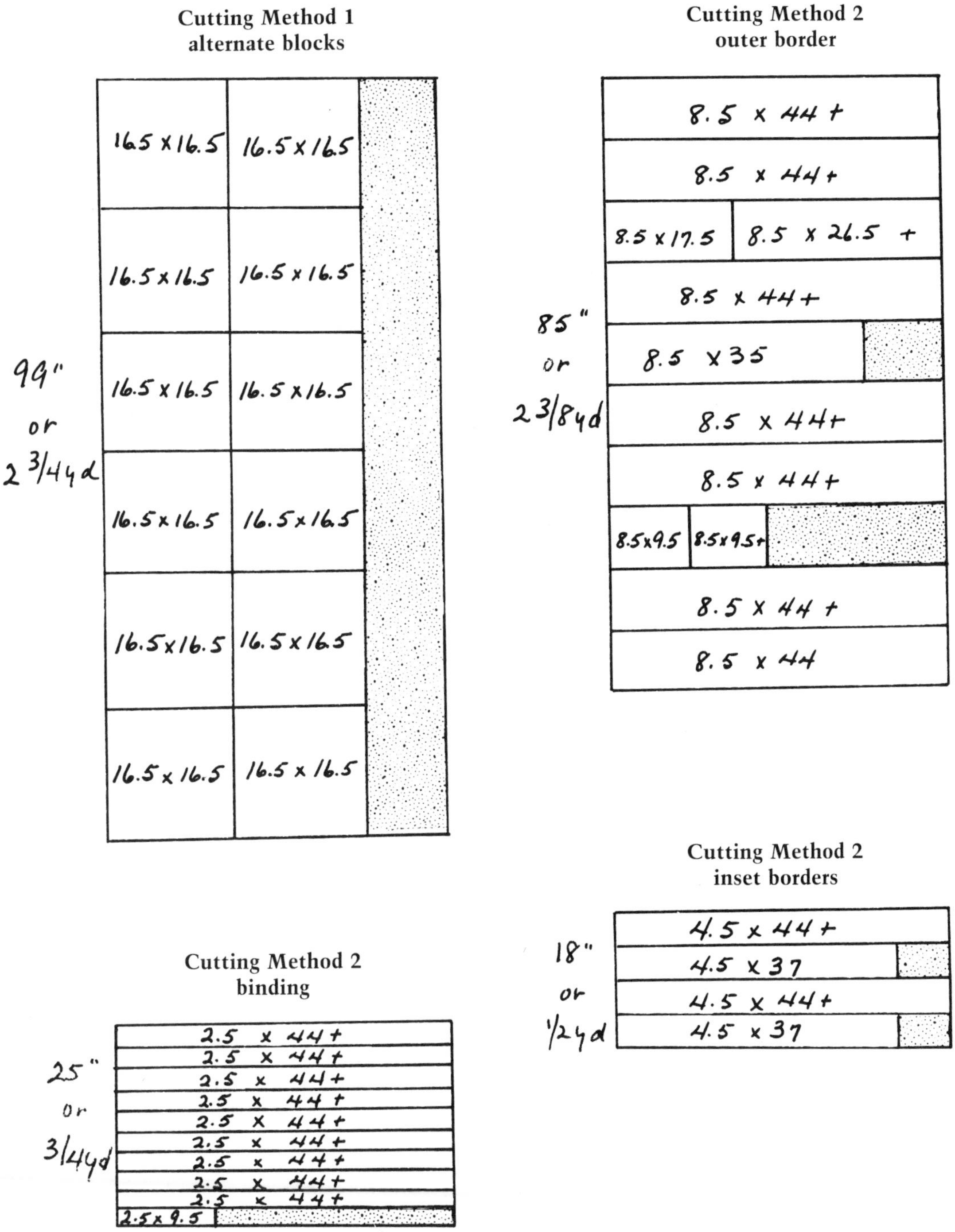

Cutting Method 1
alternate blocks

16.5 × 16.5	16.5 × 16.5	
16.5 × 16.5	16.5 × 16.5	
16.5 × 16.5	16.5 × 16.5	
16.5 × 16.5	16.5 × 16.5	
16.5 × 16.5	16.5 × 16.5	
16.5 × 16.5	16.5 × 16.5	

99"
or
2 3/4 yd

Cutting Method 2
outer border

8.5 × 44 +
8.5 × 44 +
8.5 × 17.5   8.5 × 26.5 +
8.5 × 44 +
8.5 × 35
8.5 × 44 +
8.5 × 44 +
8.5 × 9.5   8.5 × 9.5 +
8.5 × 44 +
8.5 × 44

85"
or
2 3/8 yd

Cutting Method 2
inset borders

4.5 × 44 +
4.5 × 37
4.5 × 44 +
4.5 × 37

18"
or
1/2 yd

Cutting Method 2
binding

2.5 × 44 +
2.5 × 44 +
2.5 × 44 +
2.5 × 44 +
2.5 × 44 +
2.5 × 44 +
2.5 × 44 +
2.5 × 44 +
2.5 × 44 +
2.5 × 9.5

25"
or
3/4 yd

4–16   King with skirt cutting methods.
Finished size, 96" × 104"; Arrangement, 5 × 5 block to block, single border; Block size, 16 inches square; Inset borders, 4 inches wide (top & bottom); Outer borders, 8 inches wide.
Yardage required: Alternate blocks (if desired), 2¾ yards; Inset borders, ½ yard; Outer borders, 2⅜ yards; Backing, 7½ yards; Binding, ¾ yard.

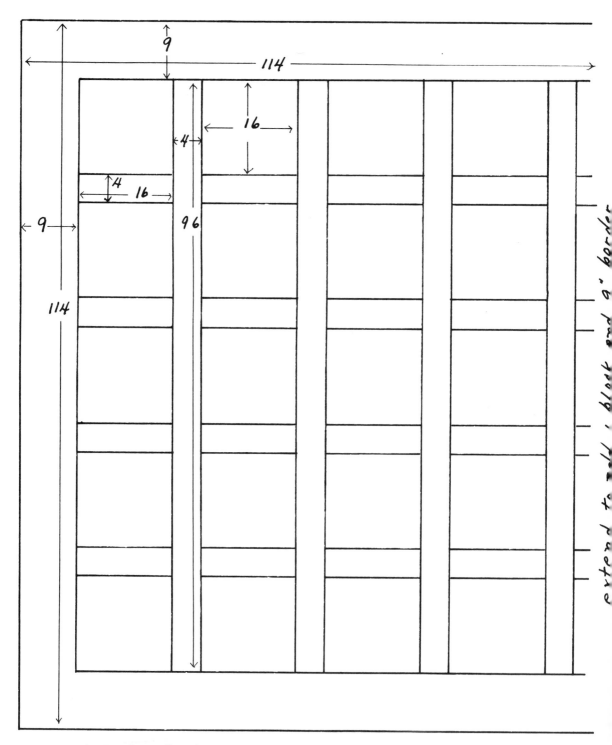

4–17 King to floor layout.

50

Cutting Method 1
sashing

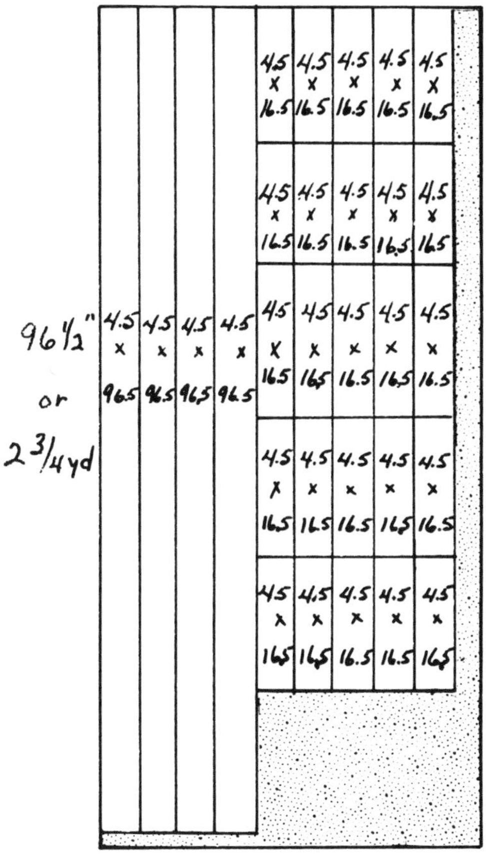

	4.5 x 16.5	4.5 x 16.5	4.5 x 16.5	4.5 x 16.5	4.5 x 16.5
	4.5 x 16.5	4.5 x 16.5	4.5 x 16.5	4.5 x 16.5	4.5 x 16.5
96½" or 2¾ yd	4.5 x 16.5	4.5 x 16.5	4.5 x 16.5	4.5 x 16.5	4.5 x 16.5
(96.5 96.5 96.5 96.5)	4.5 x 16.5	4.5 x 16.5	4.5 x 16.5	4.5 x 16.5	4.5 x 16.5
	4.5 x 16.5	4.5 x 16.5	4.5 x 16.5	4.5 x 16.5	4.5 x 16.5

Cutting Method 2
border

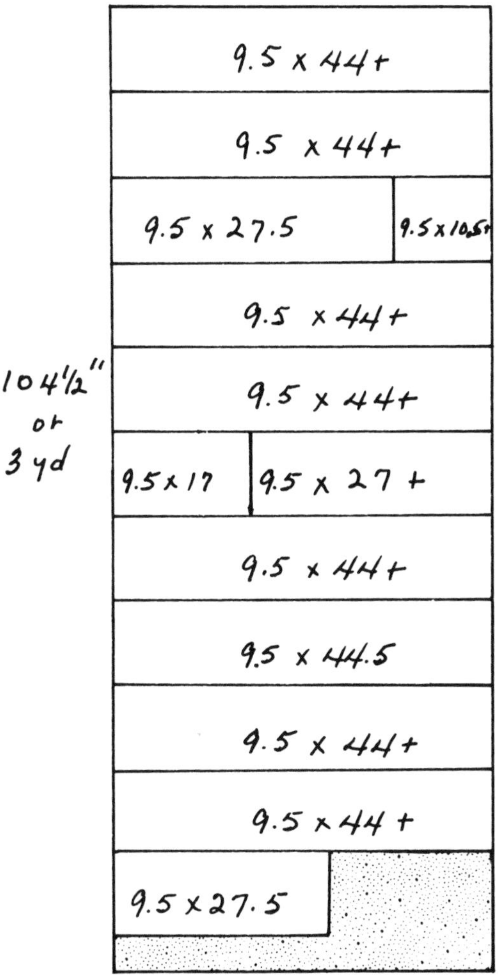

104½" or 3 yd

9.5 x 44+
9.5 x 44+
9.5 x 27.5 | 9.5 x 10.5+
9.5 x 44+
9.5 x 44+
9.5 x 17 | 9.5 x 27+
9.5 x 44+
9.5 x 44.5
9.5 x 44+
9.5 x 44+
9.5 x 27.5

Cutting Method 2
binding

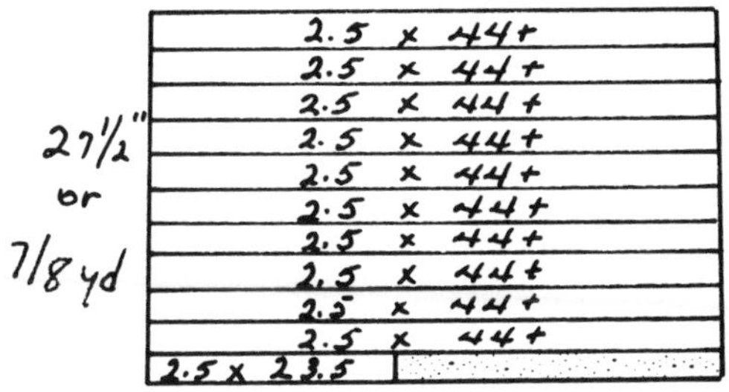

27½" or 7/8 yd

2.5 x 44+
2.5 x 44+
2.5 x 44+
2.5 x 44+
2.5 x 44+
2.5 x 44+
2.5 x 44+
2.5 x 44+
2.5 x 44+
2.5 x 44+
2.5 x 23.5

4–18 King to floor cutting methods.
Finished size, 114″ × 114″; Arrangement, 5 × 5 blocks, single border; Block size, 16 inches square; Sashing, 4 inches wide; Borders, 9 inches wide; Binding, ½ inch wide. Yardage required: Sashing, 2¾ yards; Borders, 3 yards; Backing, 11 yards; Binding, 7/8 yard.

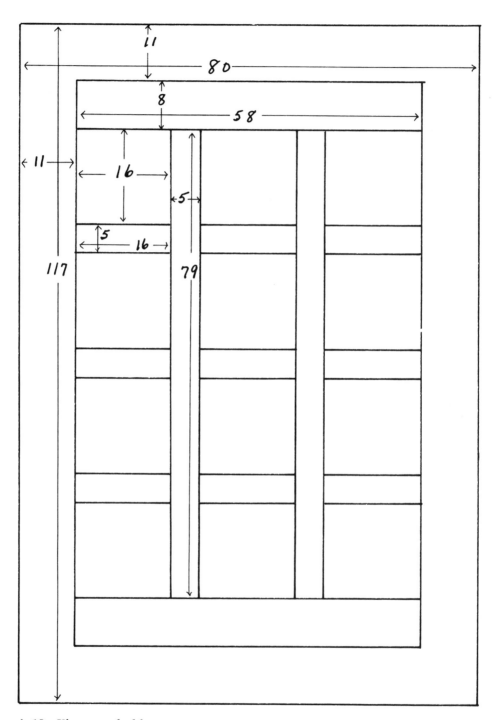

4–19 King waterbed layout.

Cutting Method 1
sashing & inset border

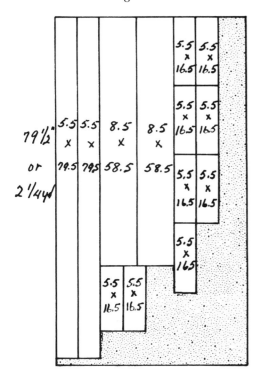

Cutting Method 2
outer border

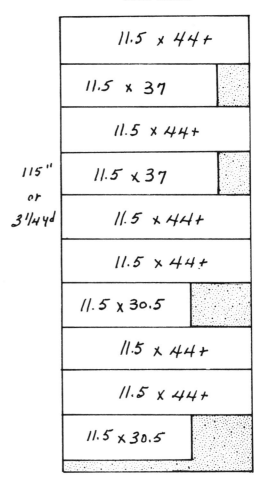

Cutting Method 2
binding

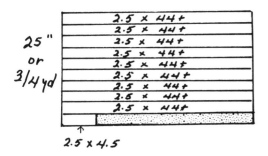

4–20   King waterbed cutting methods.
Finished size, 80″ × 117″; Arrangement, 3 × 4 blocks, single border; Block size, 16 inches square; Sashing, 5 inches wide; Inset borders, 8 inches wide (top & bottom); Outer borders, 11 inches wide; Binding, ½ inch wide.
Yardage required: Sashing & inset borders, 2¼ yards; Outer borders, 3¼ yards; Backing, 8 yards; Binding, ¾ yard.

layouts with yardage amounts for sashing or alternate blocks, borders, backing and binding. Notice that some of the layouts have a single border, others double or triple. Multiple borders are used so that the need to piece additional blocks is reduced as much as possible. This is a book on how to handle different assembly problems, not necessarily a pattern book. Choose the quilt that fits your needs most closely, or make your own layout (see Chapter 12).

Exact yardage requirements for piecing and applique are not included. Because I don't know which blocks you will choose to make or how many colors you will use, it is impossible for me to do this. Assume the block is red, white and blue. If blue is the predominant color with a little red and white, obviously more blue fabric will be needed. Therefore, you must determine which blocks you will make, how many colors you will use and where they will be placed in order to accurately judge fabric needs. As a general rule, however, you can buy for each block: ¼ to ⅓ yard of each color, if three fabrics are used; ⅛ to ¼ yard of each color, if four fabrics are used. Then multiply the above amount by the number of total blocks to be made to get the yardage required. You will need ½ yard of 45-inch material for two 16-inch background blocks.

CUTTING SASHING AND BORDERS

I prefer to cut the sashing, borders and background blocks before I start piecing my sampler blocks. There is a good reason for this. The sashing, borders and background blocks take up the greatest amounts of fabric. If, after cutting these out, you feel there might not be enough fabric left for piecing, you will have time to purchase more. As with buying yarn, you cannot depend on being able to get exactly the same shade if you have to buy it at a later date. Fabric manufacturers usually make a print for only one season (three or four months). If a print is very popular, a store may have only one opportunity to buy it. This is why it is so important for you to purchase all the fabric you need at one time.

I learned this while making my first quilt. I ran out of a solid green fabric for the binding and looked for it for three years. Since the fabric was available, I knew the color was probably still being made. Five days before I was to hang my quilt in a show I found the fabric—an exact match. After that experience, I now buy all (and more) than I need to begin with.

Fig. 1   Sampler quilt. Made by Joy Pickell. 54″ x 74″.

Fig. 2   A mockup of the sampler quilt, pinned and glued. Compare this with the finished quilt in Fig. 3 to see rearrangement of blocks and exchange of prints and solids in designs.

Fig. 3   The sampler quilt used as the example quilt-as-you-go project in this book. Made by the author. 102″ x 102″. Block patterns are, from left to right: first row—North Carolina Rose, Starred Circle, Grandmother's Flower; second row—Birds in Heaven, Young Man's Fancy, Broken Crystals; third row—Star Flower, Honey Bee, Elizabethan Flower.

Fig. 4 Honey Bee: a simple nine-patch combined with applique.

Fig. 5 Young Man's Fancy: more involved piecing is required.

Fig. 6 Elizabethan Flower: advanced applique block designed by the author.

Fig. 7 Starred Circle: a block designed by the author to incorporate all degrees of curves.

Fig. 8   Wedding Anniversary Quilt. Made by Marcelle Weigandt. 88″ x 128″.
The interior has been assembled and one inner border joined; there will be
two borders on the completed quilt.

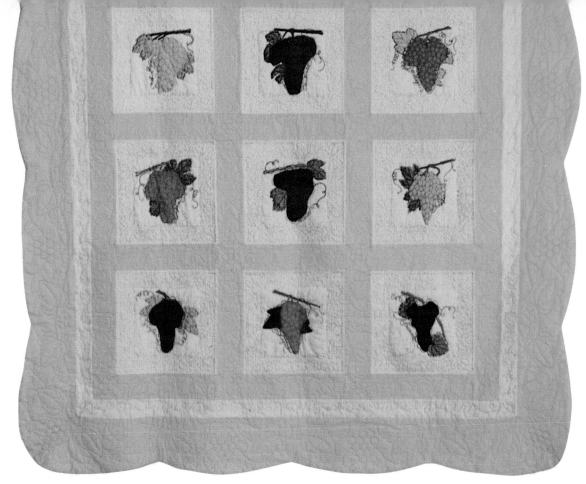

Fig. 9 Vintage San Joaquin. Made by Eula Miles and Doris Hammer. 85″ x 93″. This original design depicts wine-grape varieties grown in the San Joaquin Valley.

Fig. 10 Birds in Heaven pattern made into a pillow. Block pieced by the author and assembled by Nancy Lord.

Fig. 11 Lancaster Coun-
try Rose. Made by Jean
Bell. 102″ x 110″. This pat-
tern was published in
*Good Housekeeping
Needlecraft,* Spring-
Summer, 1977.

Fig. 12 A quilter's color
wheel, made from fabric
prints and solids; the
frame is a 14-inch quilting
hoop.

Fig. 13 Pink and white crib quilt. Made by Eula Miles. 47″ x 67″. Applique and embroidery were added to the center of the blocks.

Fig. 14 Crossed Canoes quilt with sashing; the secondary pattern forms circles. Made by Beth Simpson; owned by Dean and Karen Simpson. 84″ x 101″.

So that you will have a specific quilt to refer to, I will use the twin to the floor layout (Fig. 4–21). Study the layout. You will see that there are four sashing strips that measure 8 by 16 inches and one long sash that is 8 by 64 inches. The inner border is the same color as the sashing and will be cut at the same time. There are two strips 8 by 56 inches and two strips 8 by 80 inches.

Note: When mentioning sizes, I *do not* include seam allowances. They are finished, sewn measurements. You must mentally add the ¼-inch seams for the cutting measurements.

Determining Cutting Methods

There are two ways to cut out your fabric (Fig. 4–22). Method 1 is to cut all pieces so the longest measurement runs the lengthwise straight-of-grain (parallel to the selvage). This eliminates any piecing of the sashing or borders, but frequently uses the most fabric. Refer to Figure 4–6.

Method 2 is more economical in fabric use. The longest measurements are placed on the crosswise straight-of-grain. The long sash and the borders would be pieced, with that seam being treated as if it didn't exist. I use both methods depending on the amount of fabric waste and how much money I have to spend on fabric. Refer to Figure 4–6.

All diagrams are figured on the use of 44-inch material—washed, dried and selvedges removed. Be sure to add seam allowances when figuring yardage amounts or cutting out.

Study Figure 4–21 to see how many of each unit are required. Next compare the measurements in Fig. 4–22 for cutting the sashing and inner borders (A through F). Obviously, there is an advantage in using method 1, since you won't have to do any piecing, and it only requires buying ⅛ yard more fabric.

In cutting the outer borders (G through J) in Fig. 4–23, you can readily see, by comparing methods 1 and 2, that you have to purchase over 1 yard more material for method 1 and will have quite a bit of leftover material. You probably will be able to use it in piecing the blocks, depending on your color scheme. Even if you can't, I would still use method 1, as it means only a difference of 1 yard and has the advantage of no seam lines in the borders.

These examples are really not dissimilar. I am currently making a king-size quilt in the Crossed Canoes pattern (see Fig. 12–2). The borders are white

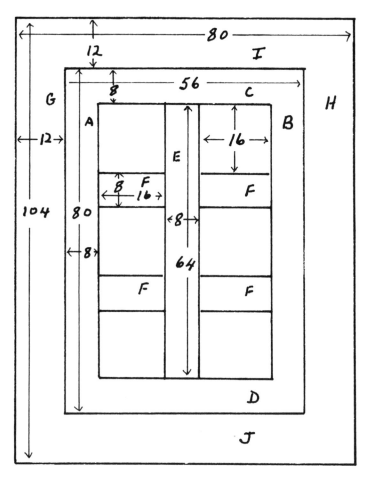

4–21 The twin to floor layout measurements are indicated in inches. A through F are sashing and inner border units. G through J are the outer border units. These are all finished measurements. The seam allowances must be added when figuring yardage and when cutting.

Cutting Method 1

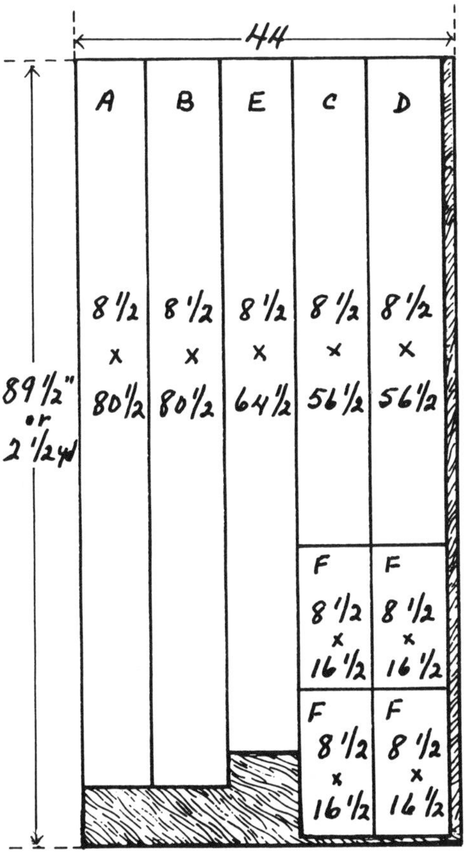

Cutting Method 2

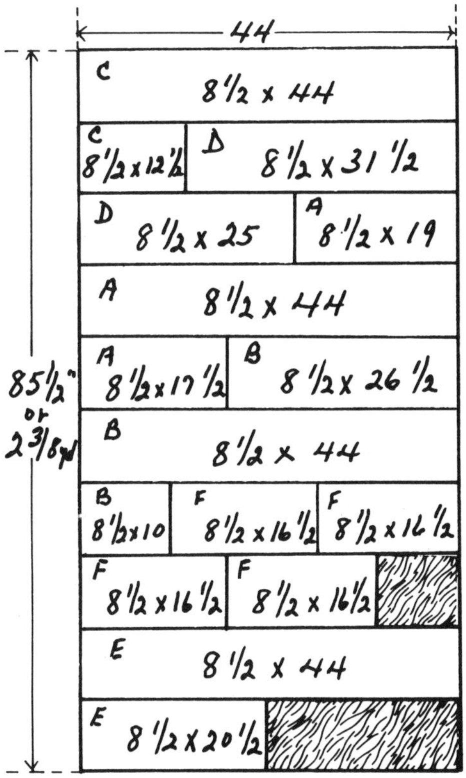

44

A	B	E	C	D

89½"
or
2½yd

A 8½ x 80½
B 8½ x 80½
E 8½ x 64½
C 8½ x 56½
D 8½ x 56½

F 8½ x 16½
F 8½ x 16½
F 8½ x 16½
F 8½ x 16½

44

C 8½ x 44

C 8½ x 12½   D 8½ x 31½

D 8½ x 25   A 8½ x 19

A 8½ x 44

A 8½ x 17½   B 8½ x 26½

B 8½ x 44

B 8½ x 10   F 8½ x 16½   F 8½ x 16½

F 8½ x 16½   F 8½ x 16½

E 8½ x 44

E 8½ x 20½

85½"
or
2⅜yd

4–22 In comparing the cutting of sashing and inner borders, it is apparent that method 1 has the advantage. The units do not have to be pieced and only a small amount of extra fabric has to be purchased.

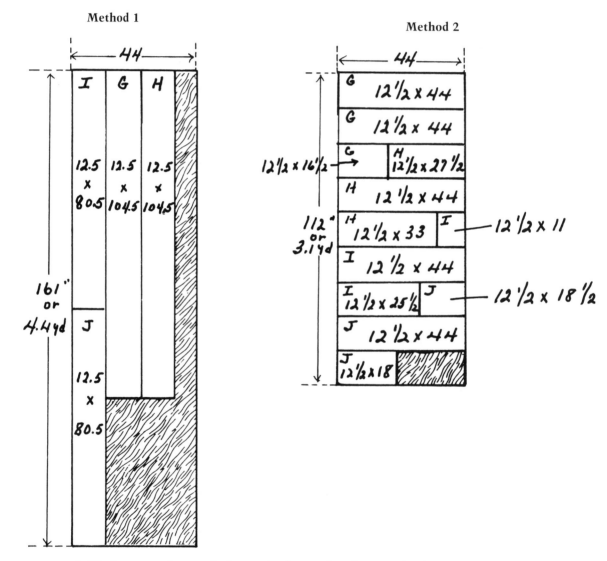

Method 1

44

| I | G | H |

12.5 x 80.5 | 12.5 x 104.5 | 12.5 x 104.5

161" or 4.4yd

J

12.5 x 80.5

Method 2

44

G 12½ x 44

G 12½ x 44

12½ x 16½ → G | H 12½ x 27½

H 12½ x 44

112" or 3.1yd

H 12½ x 33 | I — 12½ x 11

I 12½ x 44

I 12½ x 25½ | J — 12½ x 18½

J 12½ x 44

J 12½ x 18

4–23 In comparing methods 1 and 2 for cutting the outer borders, I would use method 1 even though there is slightly over 1 yard of extra material. The excess can be used in piecing.

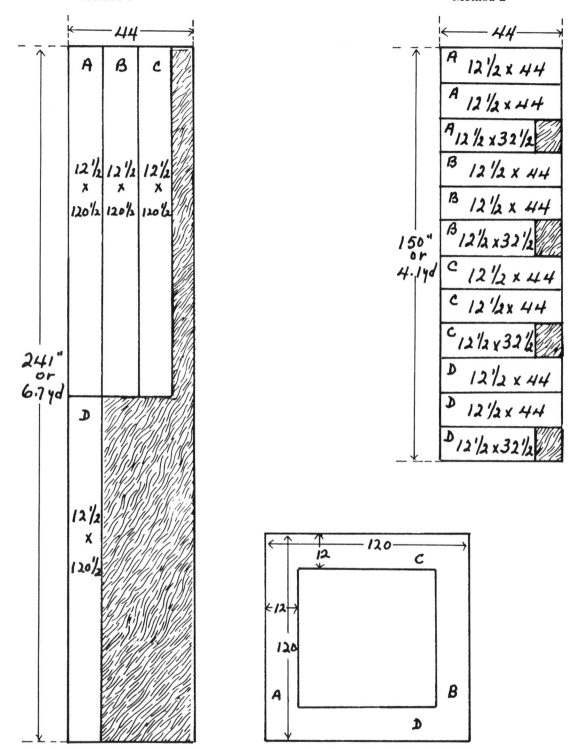

Method 1

44

| A | B | C |

12½ x 120½ | 12½ x 120½ | 12½ x 120½

241" or 6.7 yd

D

12½ x 120½

Method 2

44

A	12½ x 44
A	12½ x 44
A	12½ x 32½
B	12½ x 44
B	12½ x 44
B	12½ x 32½
C	12½ x 44
C	12½ x 44
C	12½ x 32½
D	12½ x 44
D	12½ x 44
D	12½ x 32½

150" or 4.1 yd

120

12

12

120

A

C

B

D

4–24   The cutting diagram for the border of a king-size Crossed Canoes quilt. Method 1 would not be the choice this time because of the amount of leftover fabric and the cost involved.

Top and bottom lap   **Side lap**

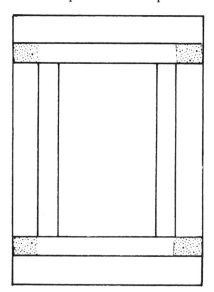 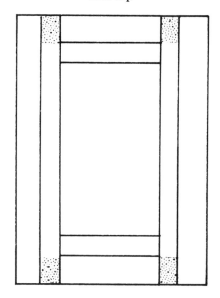

Mitered corners

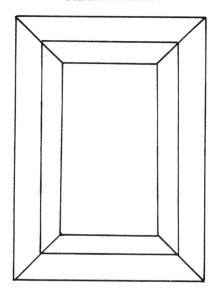

4–25 Lapped and mitered quilt corners. The shaded areas in the lapped drawings show sections that could be pieced with the outer border fabric to give a continuous band of border color.

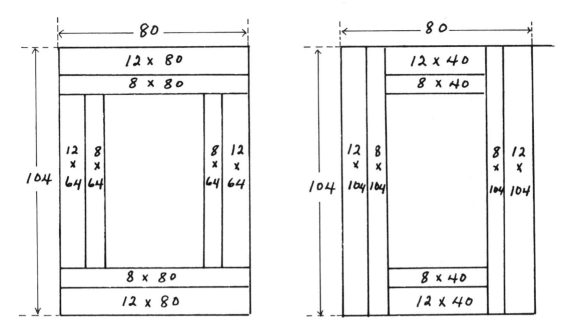

4–26 Compare the difference in these lapped measurements to the basic twin to floor measurements in Fig. 4–21.

and I didn't want to piece them. From the measurements in Fig. 4–24 you can really see a dramatic difference. Method 1 means purchasing almost twice the material, with a tremendous amount of leftover fabric. Needless to say, I chose method 2.

Sashing and Border Templates

Make a template for the sashing and borders after determining the best way to cut your fabric. For the twin to the floor layout, the sash is 8 by 16 inches. Your template can be made from Mylar, manila folders or stiff paper. I normally use artist's drawing paper because it has some body to it; yet enough light can shine through for marking quilting designs (see Chapter 9).

Make the template just as you did for the small patch templates, only work in a larger size. Lay the template on the wrong side of the fabric and trace around it with a pencil. Make sure that ½ inch is left between each pencil line for the ¼-inch seam allowances. Cut the fabric out.

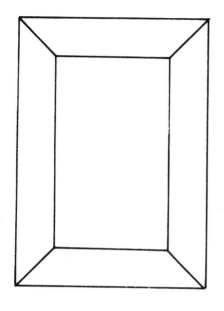

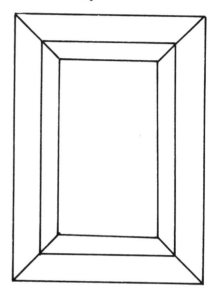

Multiple border unit

Bottom border

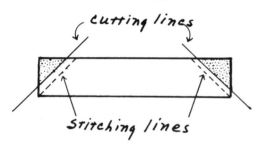

cutting lines

Stitching lines

4–27 The shaded areas indicate the excess fabric for single borders that will be cut away after the strip is quilted. This eliminates the need to baste on an extension. Be sure to leave a ¼-inch seam allowance when cutting.

Bottom border

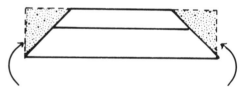

Scrap fabric extensions

4–28 The multiple mitered borders must be handled so that the strip end is squared off. Scrap fabric extensions (shaded areas) are basted onto the basted strip unit. The extension is removed after quilting.

CUTTING BORDER CORNERS

I have not yet dealt specifically with border corners. There are two ways to turn a corner: lap and miter. Your choice should be determined both by the interior design of the quilt and by personal preference. The lapped corners use a template with a squared end and the mitered borders use a template with a 45-degree angle end (Fig. 4–25).

A Log Cabin quilt pattern would use a lapped corner, because the blocks are made of narrow strips arranged so that the corners lap over each other. A quilt called Birds in Heaven (see Fig. 8–19) would have mitered corners, since the block design has 45-degree angles in the corners. If the quilt is a sampler, there are a variety of block designs, and either lapped or mitered corners could be used, whichever you prefer. The style of corner you choose must be used throughout the quilt (Fig. 4–26). The inner border should not be lapped with a mitered outer border.

The lapped border is easier to cut, since all the ends are square. Using the twin to floor layout, decide whether you want the long laps on the sides or on the top and bottom (see Fig. 4–26). Adjust the measurements on the layout accordingly and cut the borders.

Handling mitered corners is a little more difficult. You will be dealing with 45-degree angles at the strip ends. Each strip must have a straight edge to pin into the quilt-as-you-go frame, so accommodations have to be made. If the quilt is to have a single border, cut the border with a straight end. Mark the 45-degree angle stitching line on the wrong side of the fabric, just as you have for all other stitching lines. Do not cut the excess away. Assemble the strip, pin it into the frame and do the quilting. Cut the excess away after the strip is quilted and removed from the Frame (Fig. 4–27).

For a multiple border, it is best to cut away the excess material before assembling the strip. Assemble the strip with the batt and backing which are also mitered. Since you must have a straight edge to pin into the frame, an extension must be basted onto the basted strip along the 45-degree angle (Fig. 4–28). Any type of cotton-weight fabric can be used. Be sure it is basted securely to the angled cut edge. The straight edge of the extension is pinned to the frame's tape. Quilt as usual and then remove the basted fabric.

Chapter Five

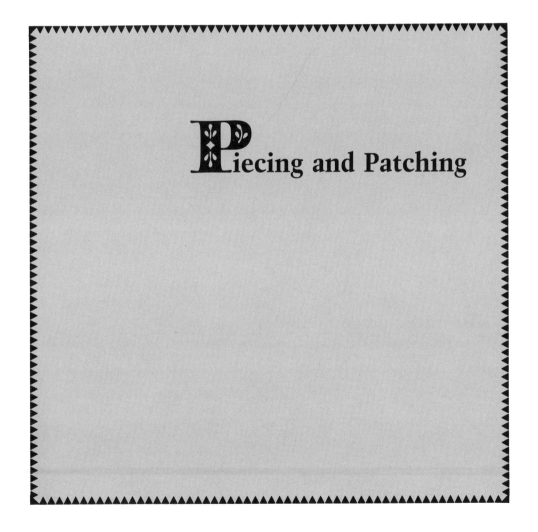

Piecing and Patching

No matter how complicated the block may be, all piecing is done in the same manner. More involved blocks simply have more patches in smaller sizes and differing shapes. Once a beginning quilter has learned the few tricks to piecing, it's full steam ahead on fancy designs!

JOINING SINGLE EDGES

Study the photograph of the completed Grandmother's Flower block in color Fig. 3 and decide how many colors you will use for the Flower and where they will be placed. Refer to Chapter 2 for color selection. Make the hexagon template and cut out the fabric patches as detailed in Chapter 3. The Flower is pieced beginning with the center hexagon, and each row of color is added in order until the Flower is as large as needed (Fig. 5–1). *Remember:* The pencil line on the patch is the stitching line; you *never* sew into the seam allowances as in dressmaking.

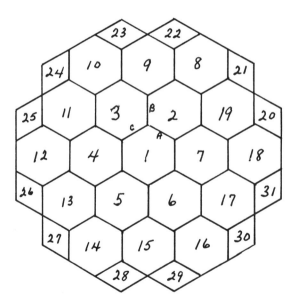

5–1 The patches should be added as they are numbered. Patch 1 forms the center and patches 2 through 7 make up row one. Patches 8 through 19 are row two. Diamonds 20 through 31 do not have to be used unless desired. (*See* Joining Multiple Edges, page 71.)

Place patches 1 and 2 with their right sides together. Pin straight into the *exact* pencil line corner of one patch and through the fabrics so that the pin comes out the other patch at its *exact* penciled corner (Fig. 5–2). Bring the pinpoint back up through the fabric on both pencil lines.

Pin the other end of the seam line in the same manner (Fig. 5–3). Notice that the pin heads are at the corners and that the sharp ends point toward the middle of the seam. If the patch is long, additional pins will be needed in the middle of the seam line. Be sure the pins are on the pencil lines of *both* patches.

Sewing Straight Seams

You are now ready to sew the first seam. Cut a thread about 18 inches long and knot it; use a single thread with a small knot. All thread is twisted and placed onto the spool so that there is less friction in sewing if the cut end is knotted. Hold the two patches firmly, close to the pin, between thumb and forefinger. Remove the pin and bring the needle up from the back patch so that the tip of the needle is about ⅛ inch in from the corner and on the pencil lines. Pull the thread through so that the knot is firmly against the back patch (Fig. 5–4). Now put the needle point into the *exact* corner of the top patch, making sure it comes out at the *exact* corner of the back patch. Angle the needle forward so that it comes up on the pencil lines between the corner and the thread knot (Fig. 5–5). Pull the thread through and taut. In simple terms, you have made a backstitch at the corner. You may feel this is not necessary, but I believe it provides a little extra stability at the corners.

To sew the main portion of the seam, run the needle in and out of the fabric on both pencil lines until there are four or five stitches on the needle (Fig. 5–6). I can't stress enough how important it is to sew on the pencil lines of *both* patches. Before you pull the needle through, turn the patch over and make sure that the needle is on the pencil line of the back patch (Fig. 5–7). If it's not, pull the needle out and shift the patches until the pencil lines are exactly aligned. You must always check this, since poor alignment now will produce an inaccurate quilt.

Once you're certain of your alignment, pull the needle through and the thread taut. Quite frequently the fabric will be puckered after the needle has been pulled through. These puckers should not be left in the patch. Gently

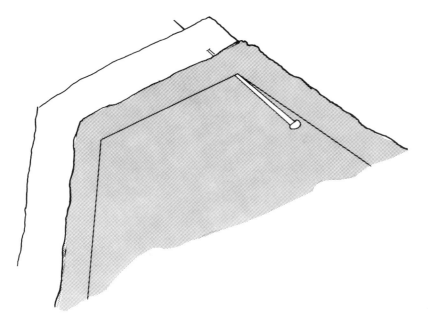

5–2 With right sides together, pin straight into the fabrics at the penciled corners.

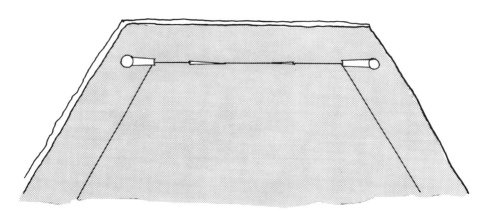

5–3 Patches are pinned together on the penciled lines.

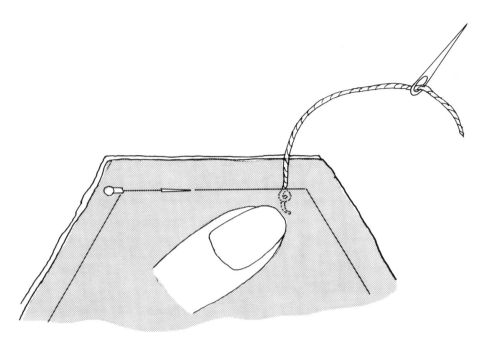

5–4 The needle is brought from the back patch about ⅛ inch in from the penciled corner.

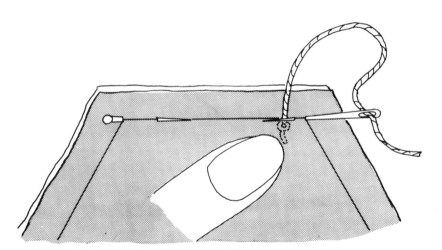

5–5 Stitch directly into the pencil corners and bring the needle back up on the lines. This will make a backstitch at the corner for extra stability.

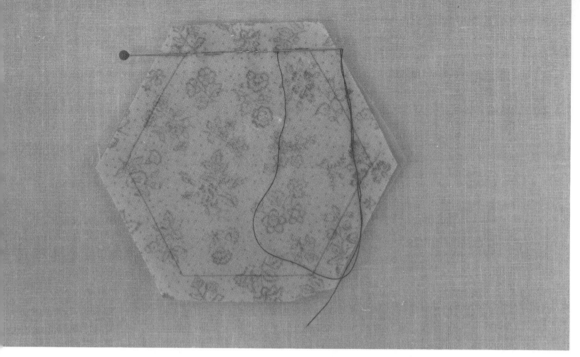

5–6 The needle is moved in and out on *both* pencil lines until four or five stitches are picked up. Stitches should be no longer than 1/16 of an inch.

5–7 Turn the patch over before pulling the needle through the fabric to see if you are on the pencil line of the back patch. If not, pull the needle out, shift the fabric and restitch.

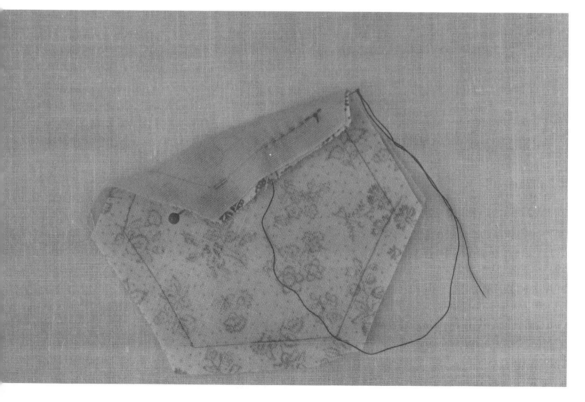

grasp the seam between thumb and forefinger and slide your fingers along the seam toward the loose end of the thread. This will remove the puckers and leave the seam flat. I do this each time I have taken four or five stitches and pulled the needle through. It should not be done at the end of the seam since it might stretch the fabric.

Continue the running stitch until close to the end of the seam. Hold the fabric firmly, remove the pin, and stitch right into the corner point. Make a small backstitch and come back up at the corner (Fig. 5–8).

To knot the thread, pick up a few threads of the patch just inside the seam allowance area and pull the thread through until a small loop is made. The loop should form a figure 8. If it has not done so, use the tip of the needle to twist the thread into an 8. Put the needle through the top loop of the figure 8 and out the bottom loop (Fig. 5–9). Pull the thread taut so that a firm knot forms. Cut the thread off, leaving a thread tail of $\frac{1}{8}$ to $\frac{1}{4}$ inch. If the thread were cut right next to the knot it might come loose. I've found that the figure 8 knot makes a very firm, tight knot, but if you prefer another type, that's okay too.

JOINING MULTIPLE EDGES (Flopping)

While it is easy to join two patches that have straight edges, it's a bit more difficult to be able to sew in two or more edges of the next patch without having to knot and cut the thread at each seam end. Patches 1 and 2 have been joined at seam A (see Fig. 5–1). Patch 3 must be joined at seams B and C. Place patch 3 over patch 2, right sides together, and pin on the pencil lines as detailed above. This time the pin on the left will be going into the *hole* where the last joining stitch was taken. *Note:* Never, at any time, are seam allowances to be sewn down. They are held up and out of the way when sewing. If the seam allowances are sewn down, they can't be moved when pressing.

Sew from the pin on the right to the pin on the left, making the backstitch through the same hole that ended the seam joining patches 1 and 2 (Fig. 5–10). If you are left-handed, reverse the directions and sew from left to right. Always sew from the outer corner to the patch center when joining multiple edges.

When you come to a seam allowance, hold it up and out of the way and poke the needle through it right at the stitching line. Pull the needle and thread

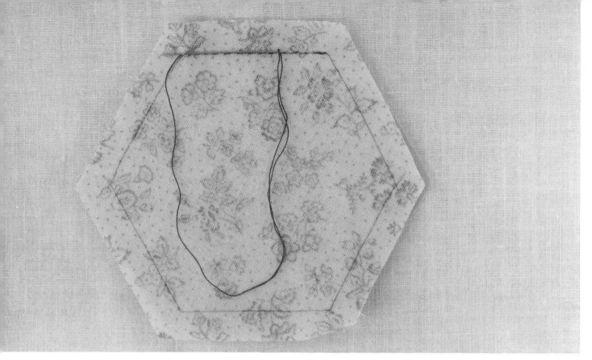

5–8   When ending the row, make a backstitch right into the corner of the patch for added strength.

5–9   To make a knot, put the needle through the top of a figure 8 thread loop and bring it out the bottom loop.

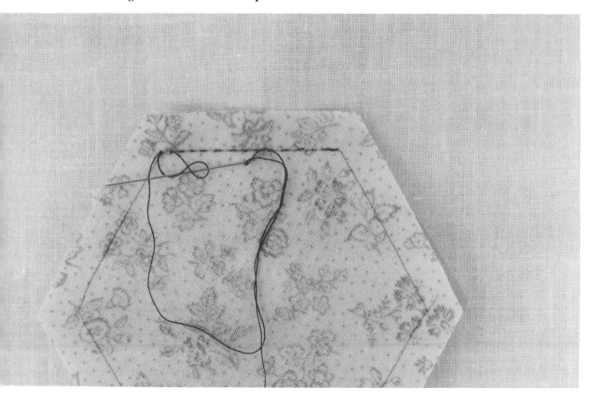

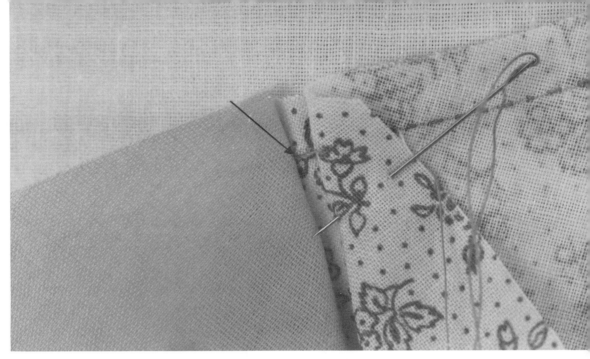

5–10 Sew up to the seam corner and make a backstitch right into the hole where the last stitch was taken to join patches 1 and 2. The patch edge has been folded back to show this.

5–11 The needle is put through the seam allowance at stitching-line level. This leaves the seam allowance free to be moved when pressing.

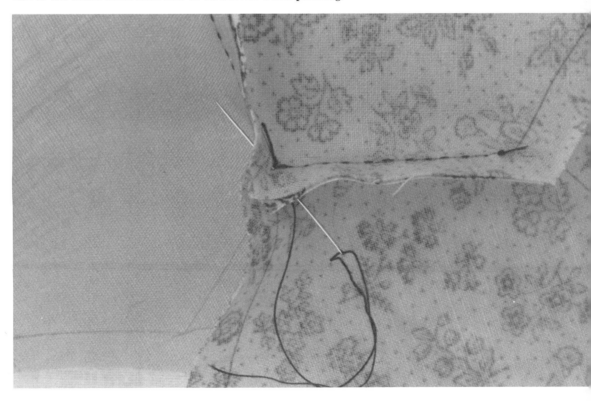

out the other side of the seam allowance (Fig. 5–11). In this manner, you have sewn from one patch to another, but not into the seam allowances. They are still "moveable."

I call this method of sewing multiple edges "flopping." First, one seam line is pinned and sewn; then the needle is run through the seam allowance to the other side and a backstitch is made (Fig. 5–12). Second, the end seam corner is pinned and sewn (Fig. 5–13). It would not only be very awkward to try to pin all the edges to be sewn at once; it would also produce a sloppy looking block. Using the "flopping" method, two or three edges of a square may be sewn into a block without cutting a thread.

Continue to add each patch in order. The last patch to be added in the first row (7) will be flopped and sewn on three edges. In the outer row of patches (8 through 19), every other patch is sewn on three edges (see Fig. 5–1).

The small diamonds (20 to 31) are added by using the same "flopping" technique. You may decide not to use the diamonds at all. In that case, the Flower is ready to press.

PRESSING

Proper pressing is as important for an accurate quilt as proper piecing. Notice that I said *pressing*, not *ironing!* Pressing is a gentle action with a soft touch and as little back-and-forth motion with the iron as possible. It is very easy to stretch those tiny bias pieces of fabric and undo all that careful cutting and piecing.

Any iron can be used, either steam or dry. A number of years ago I got tired of my steam iron burping out brown spots on the fabric. I gave that iron to my sons to hot wax their skis and bought myself a dry iron and a spray bottle for water. I never use a steam iron, but do use a pressing cloth if I have a fabric that becomes shiny when pressed. Be sure to select the correct temperature for the type of fabric.

Seams in quilting are *never* pressed open, but to one side. If the seams are pressed open, as in dressmaking, the thread is exposed to extra tension and wear (Fig. 5–14a). When seams are pressed to one side, the top patch will roll over the bottom patch very slightly and protect the seam thread (Fig. 5–14b).

When piecing, it is best to press as you go. I generally piece similar units

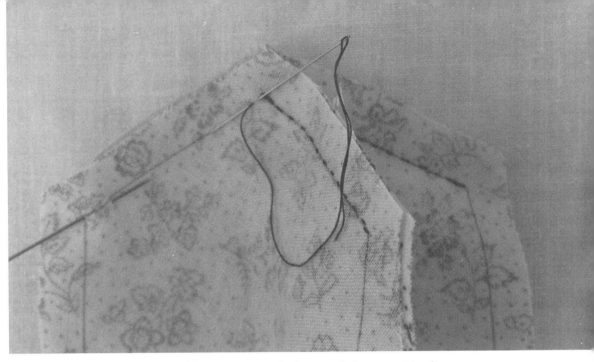

5–12   Flop the patch you are adding up to match the penciled corner. Pin that corner and back-stitch at the corner you just stitched through.

5–13   Continue sewing the seam line and end the thread as usual by backstitching and knotting.

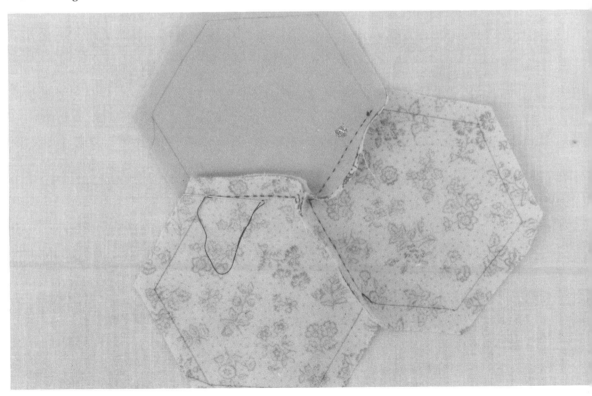

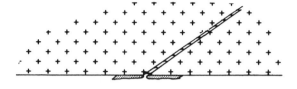

5–14a If patch seams are pressed open, the thread is exposed to friction and additional tension.

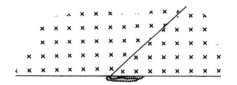

5–14b Seams pressed to one side make the top patch roll over the bottom patch, thus protecting the thread.

in a block design, stop, press them and then continue piecing. It makes the pressing and piecing easier, especially if you're working on a block with lots of tiny pieces. And the end product will look more finished.

With the Flower, I suggest piecing the center (1) and the first row (2 to 7), then pressing before continuing the piecing. Lay the pieced unit, seams up, on the edge of the ironing board with part of the unit hanging over the edge. This allows only one area to be pressed and simplifies the job (Fig. 5–15). Press the center patch (1) so that the seam allowances lay flat and are not folded back onto the patch. At the same time, the seams in the first row are pressed so that they all go in the same direction (Fig. 5–16).

A general rule to follow when pressing a block is to try not to turn the allowances toward each other, especially if they are very close, as in a diamond point. In very complicated blocks this may not be possible, and you may even have to change direction of the seam midway on the seam line, but do this only if there is no other alternative.

Now rotate the unit so that the area already pressed hangs off the ironing board and finish the pressing. Turn the block right side up and re-press each seam. This is very important since the seams have frequently overlapped each other (Fig. 5–17).

Continue piecing the outer row of patches (8 to 19) to the unit that you

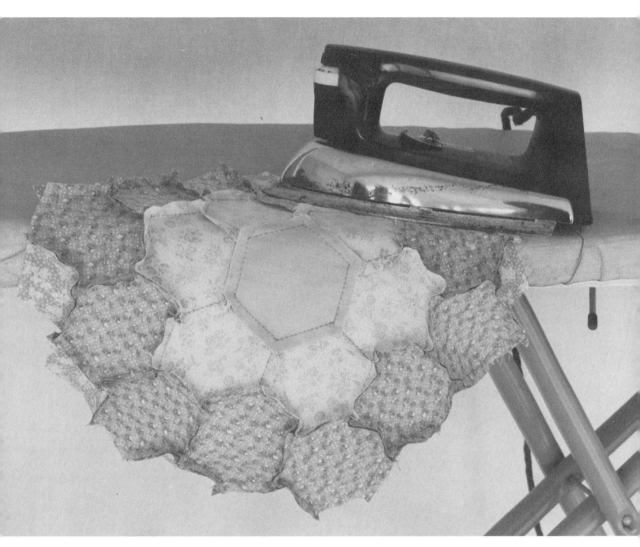

5–15 Place the block, or section of it, wrong side up on the ironing board. Let part hang over the edge so that only a small part is ironed at any one time.

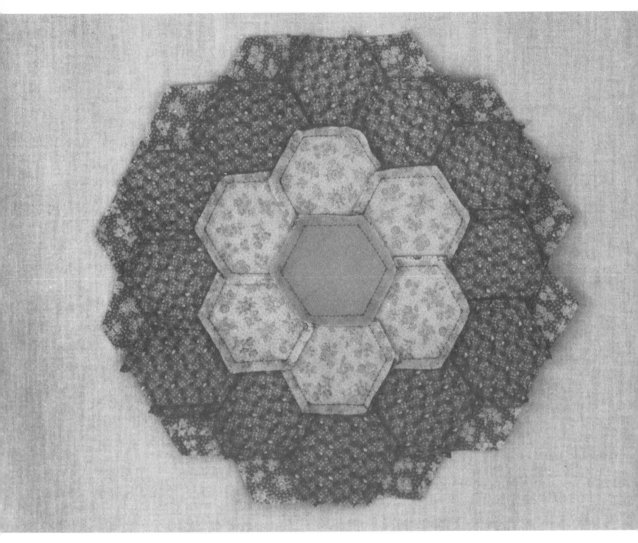

5–16   The center hexagon
is pressed flat, and the first
row is pressed so that all
the seams lay in the same
direction.

5–17 Turn the unit right side up and re-press each seam. Frequently the seams overlap and this must be eliminated.

5–18 A pleat will be formed when pressing the diamond at its corner.

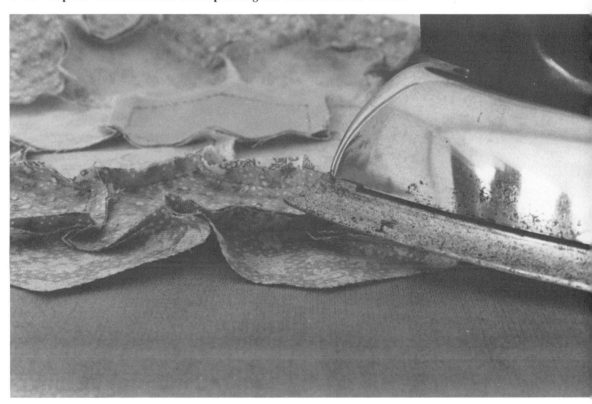

5–19   Place the needle on the pencil line and fold the seam allowance over the needle. Hold the folded seam in place and remove the needle.

5–20   Place the needle on the converging pencil line and fold that seam allowance over. Remove the needle and baste the seam allowances.

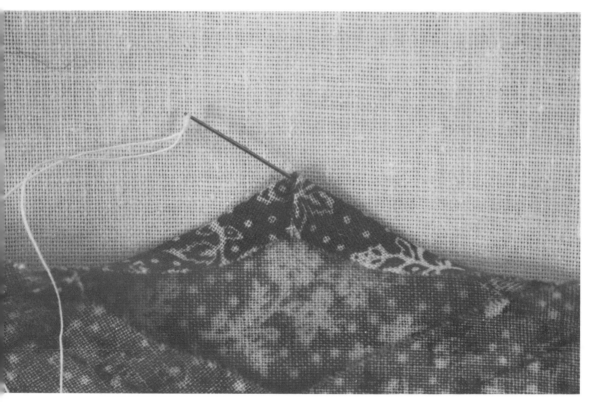

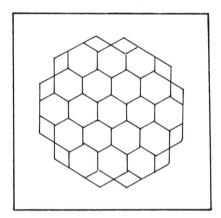 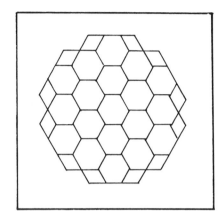

5–21 The Flower may be placed on the background block either with the points up and down or the straight edges aligned with the background block edges.

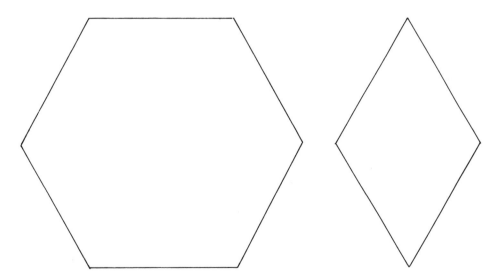

5–22 Pattern for Grandmother's Flower Garden with Diamond.

just pressed. When completed, the seam allowances should be pressed in the same direction as the first row you pressed. Piece the diamonds to the unit, and press them so that a pleat forms at the point of the diamond where it joins the two hexagon patches (Fig. 5–18).

BASTING

The Flower has now been pieced and is almost ready to be appliqued to the background block; however, the outer, raw edges must first be turned under on the pencil lines and basted down. Since the pencil lines are on the wrong sides of the patches, you will need to peek under the edges as you turn them to make sure the fold is on the line. As you turn under the seams, baste them in place with white thread (basting thread, if you have it). Don't use colored thread, as it may leave dye marks when pulled out. To get a nice, sharp turn at a corner, place the needle right on the pencil line and fold the fabric over the needle (Fig. 5–19). Hold the seam in place and remove the needle. Now put the needle along the pencil line on the next edge, and fold that seam allowance down (Fig. 5–20). Baste in place. Continue to baste around the entire Flower.

Contrary to every book you've ever read about applique, do not press the basted edges! If they are pressed down, any basting inaccuracy will be "nailed" in. I would then defy anyone to try to make a correction, short of removing all basting and starting over. Using my method of applique, you will never press any applique, and only on the Grandmother's Flower Garden and Star Flower blocks will you even do any basting. Trust me. It might take you a little longer to learn, but it will really increase your applique speed and, more importantly, you will produce really fine applique.

Chapter Six

Researchers believe that the first pieced quilts were made of patches of all the same size and shape. Certainly, it would have been easy and fast to cut out similar shapes from scrap fabric and sew them together. But I can imagine that, after making several of these, a woman might have become bored with such a necessary, repetitious occupation and might have tried to make it more interesting. Since her color selection was probably very limited, she may well have decided to create more interest by cutting the simple shapes apart into various new units, which may have developed into the patterns we are familar with today (Fig. 6–1).

Because the unit divisions in Fig. 6–1 are easy to make by folding paper

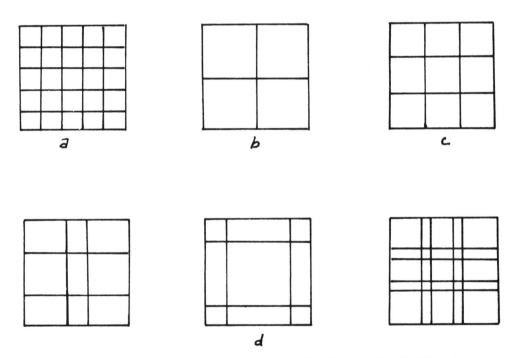

6–1 (a) Simple repeat, square block arrangement; (b) "four patch," dividing the square into four equal divisions; (c) "nine patch," the block divided into 9 equal divisions; (d) "nine patch," the block divided into 9 unequal parts.

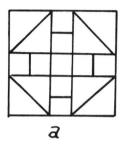 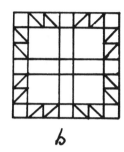 

6–2   (a) **Five-unit division, Monkey Wrench pattern;** (b) **seven-unit division, Bear's Paw pattern;** (c) **diamond division, Lemoyne Star pattern.**

or fabric, they probably formed the basis for the first quilt blocks. As more creative hands worked at quilting, block divisions became more complicated and more difficult to draw and cut accurately. The blocks in the following figures are divided into five and seven units (Fig. 6–2). Diamond patterns can be the most involved to draft accurately and fall into their own classification.

In any of the block categories in Figures 6–1 and 6–2, each of the small units can be divided into smaller shapes to give an infinite variety to a block design. Even so, that block would still keep its original classification. It is important to note that some blocks have so many divisions that it may be difficult to decide just which group they fall into (Fig. 6–3).

In this chapter we will discuss piecing a basic "nine-patch" combined with an easy applique design, the Honey Bee. Regardless of the shape of the patches, all piecing is done as described in Chapter 5, Figures 5–2 through 5–13. For that reason, in this and succeeding chapters, I will only deal with specific problems in constructing a block.

METHODS OF ASSEMBLY

Once you have become comfortable with the mechanics of piecing, each new block design offers a challenge in choosing fabrics and colors as well as in their placement and block assembly. If three people piece the same block,

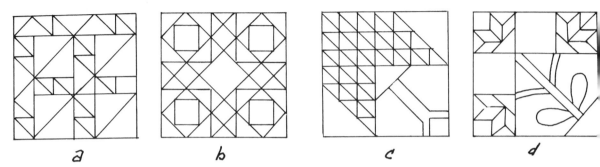

6–3 Blocks with many patches still fall into basic categories: (a) "four patch," Mixed T; (b) "five patch," Joseph's Coat; (c) "seven patch," Pine Tree; (d) "nine patch," Noon Lily.

they each may put it together in a different order. All would be correct, but one way might be the easiest. Study each block and try to determine which way will be the easiest for you. In the simpler blocks, such as Honey Bee, logic tells us all to assemble the patches in the same way. Refer to Fig. 6–4 for the Honey Bee assembly. (See color Fig. 4)

In more complicated blocks, like Young Man's Fancy, a "five-patch," there can be more than one way to assemble. The method I have diagrammed is the

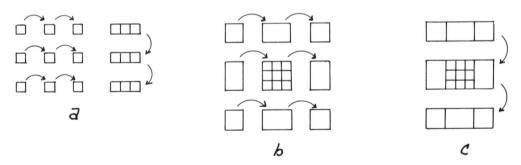

6–4 The Honey Bee assembly: (a) joining the center "nine patch," (b and c) joining the entire block.

easiest for me (Fig. 6–5), but after studying the block, you may find one or two other choices. Study color Fig. 5.

To simplify piecing, I would recommend that all like units be assembled at the same time. For Young Man's Fancy, first piece all the triangular units, then the four "nine-patches" and, last, the four rectangular units. Finally, as shown in Fig. 6–5, join the small square units into rows and then these rows into the completed block.

Whichever method used to join the blocks, all corners should meet perfectly and all seam allowances should be movable for pressing. Refer to Figs. 5–10 to 5–13.

SIMPLE APPLIQUE: THE HONEY BEE
The applique of the honey bees (leaf shapes) to the block should be done only after the piecing of the entire block is completed. Attempting to applique

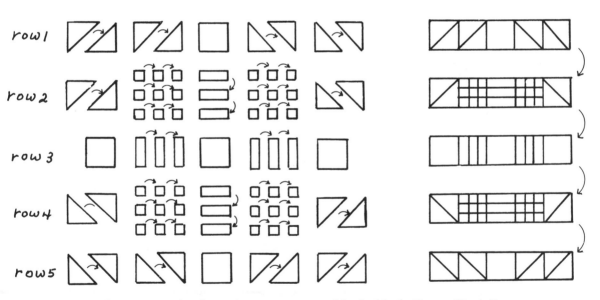

6–5   This seems to be the easiest way to assemble the block, Young Man's Fancy.

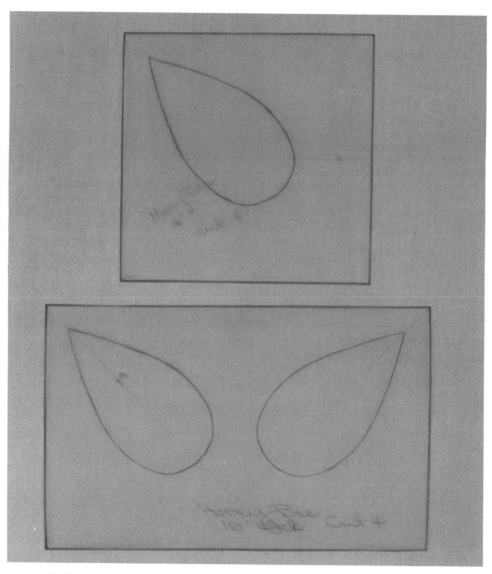

6–6 The finished Mylar template for Honey Bee. The master is made from this pattern. (The edges have been outlined for photographic clarity.)

6–7 **The master pattern for Honey Bee applique.**

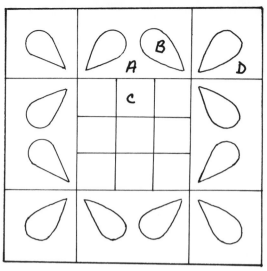

6–8 The actual sized patterns for the Honey Bee block. Remember, no seam allowances are included. They are allowed for when cutting out the fabric patches.

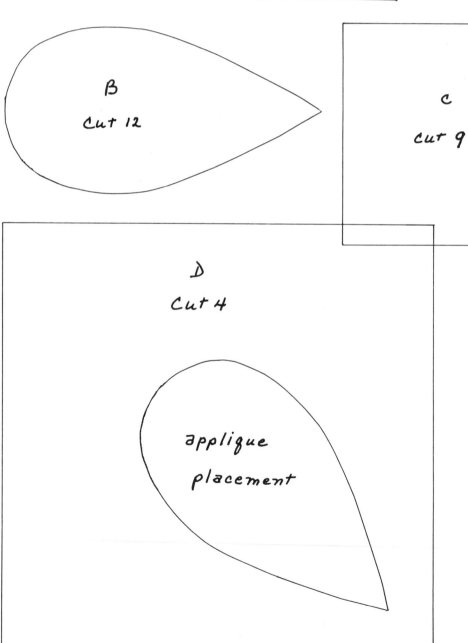

B
Cut 12

C
Cut 9

D
Cut 4

applique

placement

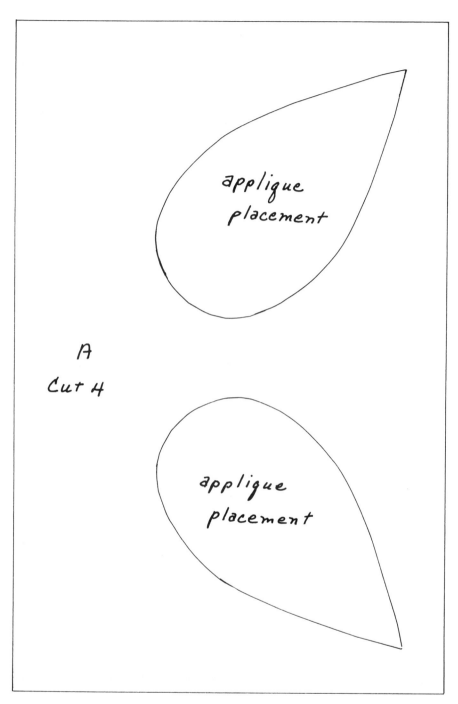

A

Cut 4

applique placement

applique placement

6–8 *continued*

onto small patches might result in pulling the fabric out of shape. Besides, it's just plain easier to handle the larger block.

Note: Marking for the applique locations, however, should be done *before* any block assembly occurs. The order is: mark and cut out the patches, mark applique lines on the necessary patches, assemble the block, applique where needed.

In Grandmother's Flower Garden, the Flower was positioned in the center of the block and checked by ruler to make sure that it was properly aligned. Because you were only dealing with a single finished shape on a single background, that method was adequate. The Honey Bee is a different matter.

SIMPLE MASTER PATTERN

There are six leaf shapes to be appliqued onto six background patches. If you used the "plunk and pin" method favored in most books on applique, you would not have each of the six shapes in exactly the same finished size, pointed in exactly the same direction or positioned in exactly the same spot. To me that is very important; it should be to you, too.

There is a very simple, effective way to handle applique in this situation. On each of the patch templates that has an applique, draw the finished-size design in the exact location you want it. This has been done for you on the Honey Bee pattern (Fig. 6–8). Do not include the seam allowances. Cut out the template (Fig. 6–6) as usual. Make a copy of your template from typing paper or paper of a similar weight. Duplicate the leaf design by laying the paper over the template and tracing over the leaf shape. Go over this penciled line with dark, felt-tip pen; a ball-point pen might smear. You have just made a very simple paper master pattern (Fig. 6–7).

Place the paper master pattern on the *wrong* side of the fabric patch, being careful to match its edges to the penciled stitching lines. Pin in place. Tape this small, pinned unit to the window (paper touching glass). The right side of the fabric is facing you. The light will shine through the fabric well enough that you will be able to see the darkened pencil line. This will be the stitching line for the applique, so make sure it is a clear, unbroken line. Refer to Figs. 7–6 and 7–7. Press down with your pencil just hard enough so that you can

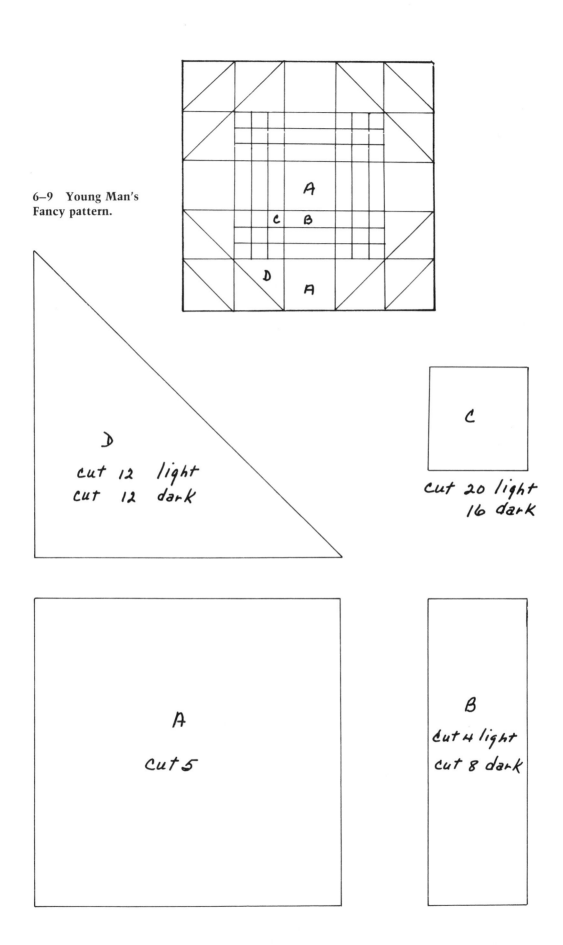

6–9   Young Man's
Fancy pattern.

A

C   B

D

A

D
cut 12 light
cut 12 dark

C
cut 20 light
16 dark

A
cut 5

B
cut 4 light
cut 8 dark

distinguish the line. It takes some practice, since you can't really see the line as you draw it because of the dark pen line underneath. Try it out on a scrap of fabric first. If you are using a white or light colored fabric, the marking can probably be done on a tabletop. For a more detailed explanation of this technique and for the actual Honey Bee applique instructions, see Chapter 7.

Chapter Seven

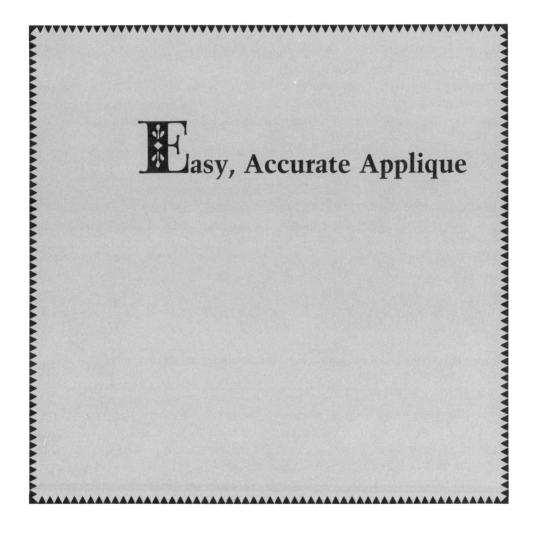

Easy, Accurate Applique

Applique—to me, the most exciting, creative, fast, satisfying needle-and-thread technique. To many, the most frustrating, time consuming and difficult task they ever tried.

Everything written about applique tells you to work the same way: trace around the template, cut out the fabric, baste the edges under, press, plunk down, pin in place, applique. Using my method you will make a master pattern, make the template, trace around the template, cut out the fabric, place the master pattern on the background fabric, pin the patches in place (if desired) and applique. Notice that in my method you do not do any basting or pressing and you are appliqueing to a pattern.

I want to briefly review the traditional applique method so that you understand the differences in the two methods; I then want you to promptly forget the traditional method and try the master pattern technique.

TRADITIONAL APPLIQUE

A template is made. For purposes of illustration, we'll call it a tulip design. It is placed on the *right* side of the fabric and is traced with a pencil. This is the actual, finished size of the flower. The tulip is cut out, leaving a ¼-inch seam allowance outside the pencil line. The seam allowance is turned under on the pencil line and basted in place. The basted tulip is pressed. It is then placed on the background block and moved around until it looks as if it is positioned accurately. The fabric tulip is pinned in place and appliqued. The basting threads are removed.

Let's look at some of the problems in the above method. Because the tulip design is traced onto the right side of the patch, the pencil lines are often visible at the edge of the patch, even after appliqueing. Next is basting: basting stitches should be fairly long, but it is almost impossible to take even ¼-inch stitches around the curved tulip base and get a smoothly turned edge. What you will get is a series of little points on the curve. The patch is then pressed, effectively locking in all the little points. Now you must position the patch by using the "plunk and pin" method. There may be no problem if it is only one tulip on a single block; but what if you are making twelve blocks with three tulips each? It is humanly impossible to be accurate on each of the twelve blocks. That is important to me! If the quilt is all the same block design, I want all the blocks to be the same! Finally, the tulip is pinned in place and appliqued.

MASTER PATTERN APPLIQUE

Because of the problems discussed, I developed the master pattern technique. It is my hope that this method will produce good applique with little frustration.

In almost all applique (except free-form) there is a specific design to be followed. The single-shape Honey Bee design was discussed in Chapter 6. Other designs, like the North Carolina Rose (color Fig. 3, and on the cover) or the Elizabethan Flower (color Fig. 6) blocks have more involved shapes, all of which must be positioned accurately. The circled stem in North Carolina Rose, for example, must be an exact circle, not lopsided or oval, and the leaf tips should all point the same way. The best way to assure this is to make an accurate paper pattern for your design. This way you can do all the positioning with a pencil on paper instead of fabric patches on a background block. It's a lot faster and certainly easier to make corrections with an eraser.

Drawing the Master Pattern

Cut a piece of paper to the exact finished size. Drawing paper or typing paper can be taped together to give the size you need to work with. In this book all blocks are 16-inch squares. Make sure that the square is really accurate. Begin the master by dividing the 16-inch square into four equal units. In this block it would be 8-inch squares (Fig. 7–1). Draw and cut out the shapes you have in mind, such as tulip, stem leaves, etc., in paper without seam allowances. Move them around in one of the 8-inch squares until you are satisfied with the balance (Fig. 7–2). Trace around each shape with a pencil. This completes one quarter of the master pattern. I provide the quarter masters for all the applique blocks in this book (Fig. 7–32 and 7–33).

Now fold the paper block in half along the division line, with the design lines to the outside (Fig. 7–3). Tape the folded block to a window with the penciled design touching the glass (Fig. 7–4). Trace over the lines showing through the paper so that the design is put on the adjoining quarter section.

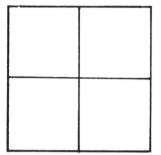 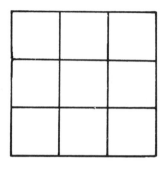

7–1 **Divide the accurate square into equal parts; these will vary, depending on the pattern.**

One-half of the master pattern is completed. Open up the 16-inch paper block and fold it horizontally on the center division line. Again, tape it to a window with the penciled design touching the glass. The design can be traced onto this half of the paper. Open up the paper block and the entire design is completed.

Check the design to see if you are pleased with it. Does it have any gaping holes where there should be a flower or leaf? Is it balanced? If you need to make adjustments, work with a quarter of the design and repeat Figures 7–3 and 7–4. When the penciled design is exactly the way you want it, carefully go over each line with a dark, felt-tip pen. Do not use a ball-point pen, as it might smear. The master pattern is completed.

You can use your master pattern for one block or a hundred. Don't throw it away when the block is finished; save it for future use. You can also make masters for the quilting designs on blocks, borders and sashing of quilts, applique designs on clothing or decorator items or for any item where a consistent pattern is needed.

Using the Master Pattern

The master pattern, for both applique and quilting designs, is used in the following manner. Cut out the background fabric in the desired shape, in this case a 16-inch square background block. Place the fabric, wrong side up, on a table. Position the master pattern, right side down, on the fabric. Align the edges of the master with the penciled stitching lines of the background block. Pin the two units together (Fig. 7–5).

7–2 Move the paper cut-
outs around until the design
is balanced. Trace each of
the shapes.

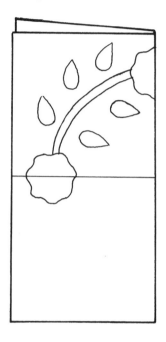

7–3 Fold the paper block in half, with the penciled design to the outside.

Tape the pinned unit to a window with the background block fabric facing you (wrong side of the paper touching the glass). Using a very sharp, soft-lead pencil, trace over the lines that are now visible because of sunlight shining through the window (Fig. 7–6). This won't work at night unless a light is directed into the window from the outside. If you have a glass-topped table, place a lamp underneath the glass and it will make an instant light box. A piece of Plexiglas stretched between two chairs or beds with a light underneath will also work well.

When tracing, one tends to scratch back and forth along the line. Try to avoid this by using your wrist as a pivot point as it rests against the fabric. Draw one fine line. As you come to the end of your reach, move your hand farther along (Fig. 7–7). Again, all traced lines must be fine, solid lines that are just dark enough to be seen. I would suggest that you make a sample before working on good fabric.

7–4 Tape the folded paper to the window so that the penciled design touches the glass. Trace over the design showing through from the other side.

7–5 Place the background block,
wrong side up, on a table and lay
the master pattern, design side
down, over it. Align the master
edges with the penciled stitching
lines of the background block.
Pin together.

7–6   Tape the pinned unit
to a window. Trace over the
master pattern lines with a
pencil. Be sure to make a
very light, single line when
marking.

right   wrong

7–7 Draw a single, fine line using your wrist as a pivot point. *Do not* scratch back and forth as you trace.

It is important to note that, at the time the master pattern is made, the quilting lines can be drawn in addition to the applique locations. A master can be made for applique only, for applique and quilting design or for quilting design only. Quilting lines should be drawn with a fine, light, solid line, not a broken line.

APPLIQUE RULES

There are several basic rules in applique that should be followed no matter how the applique is to be used.

1. Always begin with the shape most distant and work to the foreground. *Example:* to applique a sitting dog, apply the pieces in the following order: tail, hind legs, body, front legs, head, ears, nose.

2. If two pieces of applique butt against each other, the raw edge of the patch farthest away does not have to be turned under. *Example:* to applique a butterfly, sew on both wings, but do not turn under the edges that will connect to the body. Applique the body over the wing seam allowances.

3. For hand work, always use a single thread with a color that matches the fabric of the applique patch. *Example:* for a red flower on a white background block, use red thread.

4. When appliqueing a tree or flower stem and leaves, the main trunk is always appliqued last. *Example:* the smallest branches of a tree are appliqued first. The end seam allowances are then covered by the next larger branches.

This progression continues until the largest branches are sewn on, and their end seam allowances are covered by the tree trunk. In nature, the branches closest to you would join with the front surface of the trunk; with applique, however, we are dealing only with a flat surface. In addition, it's just neater to end the branches behind the trunk.

5. If possible, never start appliqueing at or near a corner, a point or at the height or depth of a curve. Try to start in an area that is as straight as possible. Of course, with a circle, it won't make any difference.

6. Use the needle as a turning tool for folding under seam allowances. Do not use your fingers.

7. *Never* trim seam allowances ahead of time. Trim only the area immediately in front of where you are actually appliqueing.

STRAIGHT LINE APPLIQUE: GRANDMOTHER'S FLOWER GARDEN

When an applique design changes fabric colors at the outer edges, as in Grandmother's Flower Garden, it is not necessary to change thread at each fabric. Choose the thread color that best matches the hexagon colors and the background color. However, if you are using strong, contrasting colors like red, white and blue, you may feel it is best to change thread at each patch. This will take a little longer, but you will be more pleased with the results.

To begin the applique, use as fine a "sharp" or embroidery needle as you can thread (see Chapter 1, under Supplies). I use a #10 "sharp" for all piecing and applique. Use a single thread, no longer than 12 to 15 inches, with a small knot. Bring the needle under the edge of the applique unit (Flower) and up to the surface, just catching the edge of the hexagon (Fig. 7–8). Insert the needle into the background fabric just beside the thread that is coming out of the applique patch. Angle the needle forward a scant 1/4 inch, bring the needle tip up through the background block and catch the edge of the applique patch. Bring the needle to the surface of the block and pull the thread taut (Fig. 7–9). Repeat the above step around the appliqued edges. At each of the hexagon corners, take a stitch right into the point; this will make a sharp corner and hold it firmly in place (7–10).

7–8   To start applique, bring the needle, with a single, knotted thread, up under the very edge of the applique patch to the surface. Pull the knot firmly against the back of the Flower.

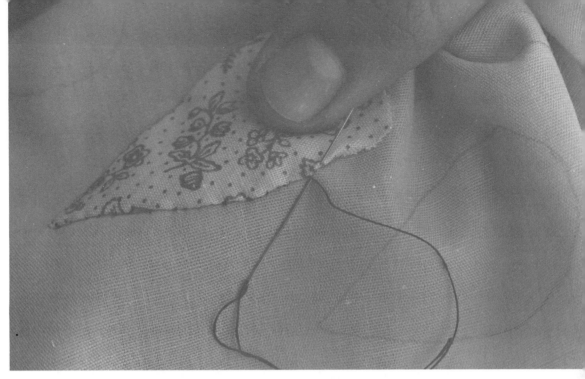

7–9   The needle tip goes into the background block directly opposite the thread coming up and out the patch, whatever its shape. Angle the needle forward a scant ¼ inch and come back up through the background block and the edge of the patch. Pull the thread taut. Repeat around the patch. A long stitch will show on the wrong side of the background block (see Fig. 7–11).

7–10   Stitch right into the corner point of each hexagon. These corners must be "nailed down."

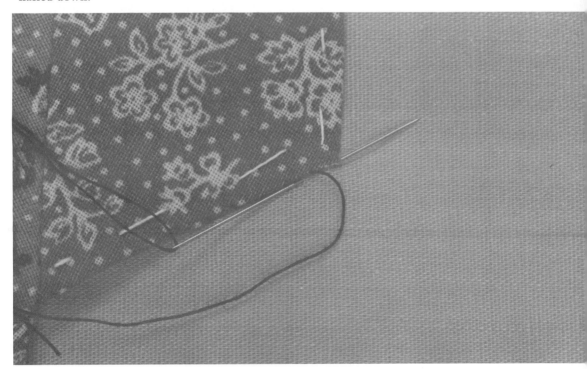

Ending Applique Threads

When the thread ends or the entire design has been sewn down, take the needle to the back of the background block and pull all the thread through. Catch a few threads of the background block, just inside the stitching line. Pull the thread enough so that a loop of about ½ inch is left (Fig. 7–11). Knot and cut the thread. Refer to Fig. 5–9 for knots.

Next, put the needle tip into the space between the background block and the Flower. Bring the tip of the needle out about ¼ inch away. Pull the thread through and cut it off at the surface of the fabric (Fig. 7–12). The thread tail will drop into the area between the background block and the Flower and be hidden. The thread tail should not be visible. This is especially important if the background block is a light color and the thread is dark. If the thread were simply cut off, the tail would be visible from the surface of the block. My method is neater! The Flower block is now completed and can be put aside until you are ready to assemble it into the strip.

INTRICATE APPLIQUE: NORTH CAROLINA ROSE

At the beginning of this chapter you used a master pattern to trace the applique design onto the background block. The individual applique patches should be cut out in the same manner as patches for geometric piecing, i.e., trace the pattern onto the wrong side of the fabric using a template and cut ¼ inch outside the pencil line to leave a seam allowance. *Note:* These pencil lines are only a guide for cutting. They are to be ignored once appliqueing begins.

Points

Remember, the actual applique stitch is the same for all applique, whether the patches are straight or curved. Refer back to Fig. 7–8 to 7–12, if you need to review.

Place the leaf patch (Fig. 7–32E) right side up over one of the leaf outlines on the prepared background block. Lift up the patch edges to make sure that it is centered and that there is adequate seam allowance on all sides. Pin the patch to the background block. Once you become adept at this applique technique, you won't need to pin small patches.

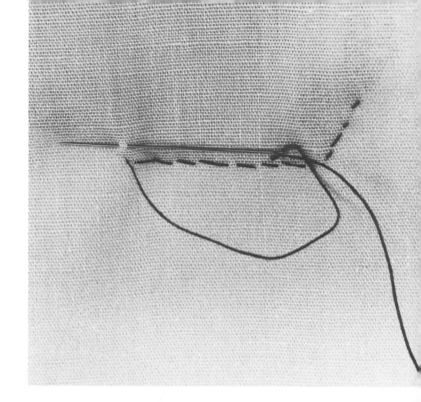

7–11 Catch a few threads of the background block just inside the stitching line. Pull the thread through until a ½-inch figure-8 loop is formed. Make a knot as in Fig. 5–9.

7–12 Weave the thread tail between the background block and the Flower for about ½ inch. Bring the thread out of the background block and cut it off at the surface of the fabric. The thread tail will drop between the two layers of the fabric and be hidden.

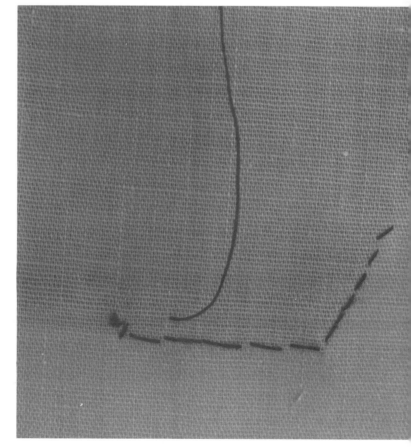

Starting on one long side of the leaf, turn under the patch seam allowance with the needle tip and sew *toward* the leaf point (Fig. 7–13). Make sure that you sew to the pencil line on the background block; this is your pattern. Ignore the line on the wrong side of the patch.

To make a sharp point, take a stitch into the patch directly over the penciled point on the background block. All the seam allowance is now pointing to the unsewn side of the leaf. Place the point of the needle into the front edge of the seam allowance and push it back into the fold of the fabric (Fig. 7–14) so that it rests against the seam line (Fig. 7–15). Take a stitch into the background block at the very point of the leaf so that it is sewn firmly in place (Fig. 7–16).

If necessary, trim away some of the top and bottom seam allowances. There should be enough fabric left to make the fold, but not enough to prevent a fine, sharp point from being formed (Fig. 7–17). Place the needle tip into the trimmed seam allowance and push it under. The side of the needle is used as a "pusher." Study Figs. 7–18 and 7–19 for this technique. Take a stitch very close to the leaf point and then continue appliqueing down the side of the leaf (Fig. 7–20).

Curves (Concave and Convex)

It is not difficult to applique a tight curve. Here are some basic rules you'll need to remember when working with curves:

1. Concave seam allowances should be clipped so the seam can stretch (Fig. 7–21).
2. Cut V shapes out of convex seam allowances to remove excess fabric when folding it under (Fig. 7–21).
3. The tighter the curve, the closer the stitches should be.
4. Seam allowances should be trimmed to about ⅛ inch, but trim only ½ inch ahead of where you are stitching.

The secret to making smooth curves is to fold the seam allowance under only about ⅓ inch ahead of the last stitch taken (Fig. 7–22). Roll the seam allowance under with the needle tip so that the edge is smooth. You may have to shift the folded seam allowance a bit to get an even curve. If there is a tiny point that won't go away, take a stitch right into its point. You'll find that the point will disappear when the thread is pulled tight.

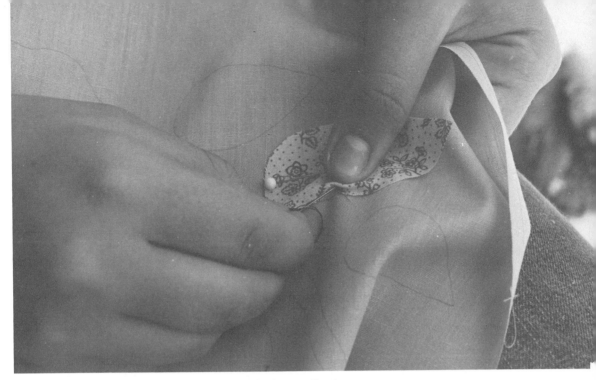

7-13   Turn the seam allowance under with the needle tip. Do not turn any seams with your fingers. It is difficult to learn, but, once mastered, will increase the speed of applique.

7-14   Use the tip of the needle to push the point of the fabric back into the seam fold of the leaf.

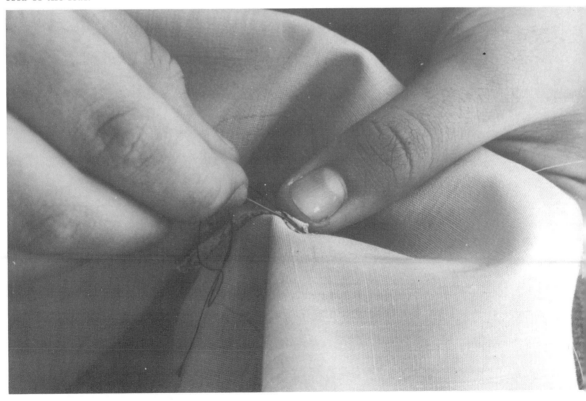

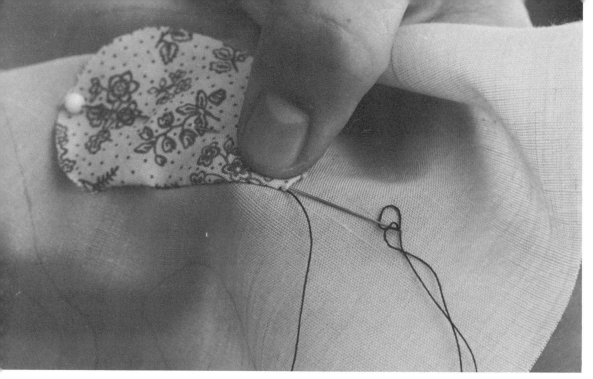

7–15 The needle will be right into the fold of the fabric.

7–16 Take a stitch into the very point and through to the background block. The leaf point will be "nailed down" in place with this stitch.

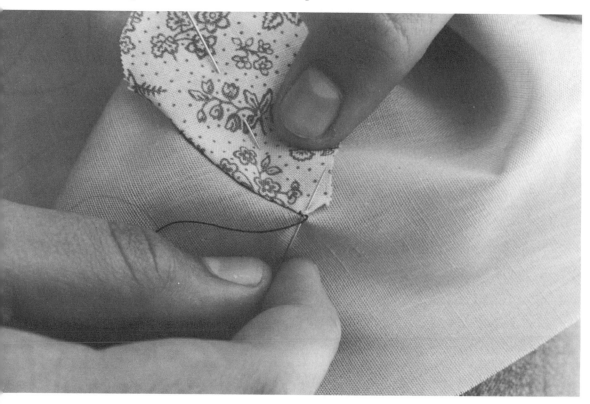

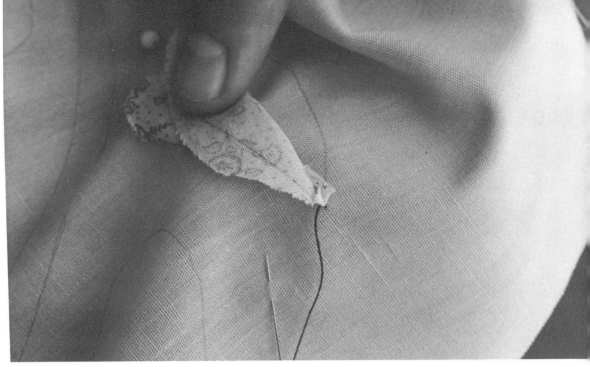

7–17   Trim the seams, if necessary. If too much fabric is left, the point will be bulky.

7–18   The fabric is shoved under with the needle tip.

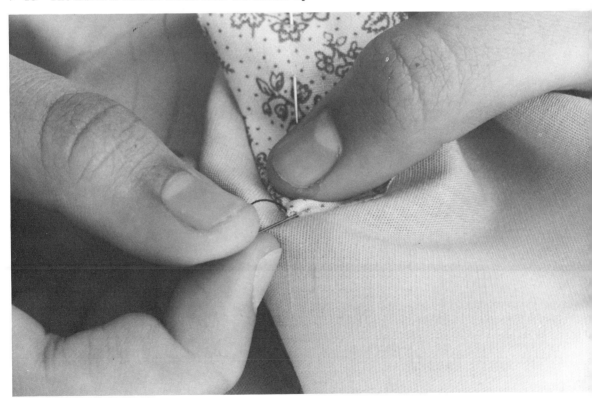

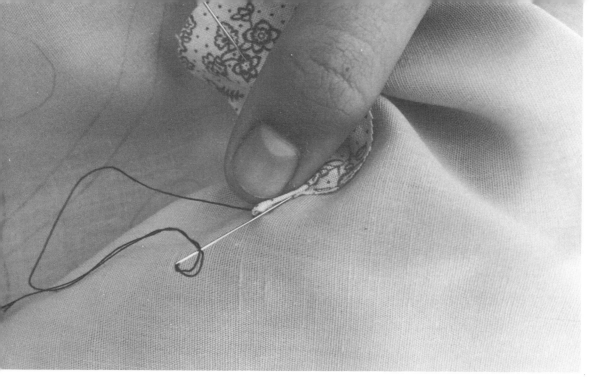

7–19   Use the side of the needle to finish pushing the seam allowance under.

7–20   Take another stitch at the leaf point and continue appliqueing down the side of the leaf. Trim excess seam allowance just ahead of where you are stitching.

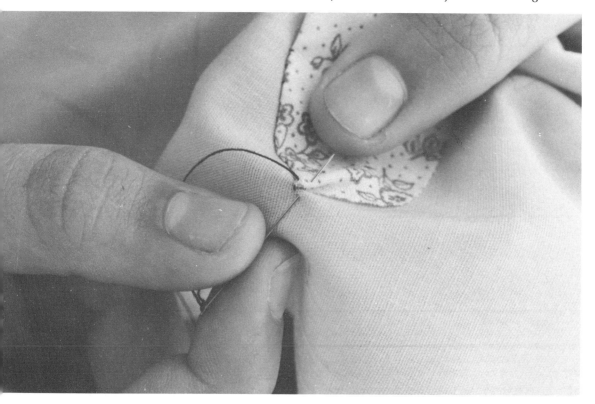

7–21 Clip concave curves and take small V shapes out of convex curves.

7–22 Only work about ⅓ inch at a time when appliqueing curves.

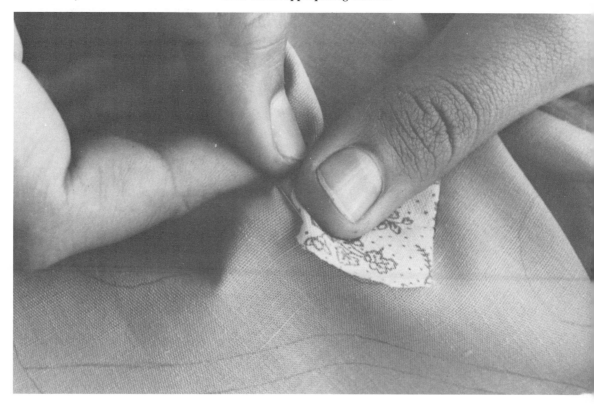

Continue appliqueing around the curve and down the side of the leaf, back to where the applique began. End the thread as directed in Figs. 7–11 and 7–12.

It may take some time for you to master the technique of handling the needle as a turning tool, but I believe you will really enjoy the speed and ease of applique once you have practiced a bit.

Straight and Curved Stems

The following techniques apply to both narrow and wide strips of fabric. If a line is even slightly curved, the fabric must be cut on the bias so that it will "move" when being sewn. The fabric may be cut on the straight-of-grain if the design is in a straight line.

Traditional Stem Applique

If stems are ¼ inch or more in width, first turn one raw edge under and applique, then fold the remaining raw edge under and applique it. You can also baste both edges under and then applique the stem one side at a time. It is important to note that, if the stem is curved, the inside curve must be sewn first (Fig. 7–23). If the outside curve is sewn first, the inside curve will pucker.

You are using a master pattern with this applique and are sewing to pencil lines. Do not baste under the seam allowances on the fabric strip. If basted, the fabric won't be adjustable.

Nontraditional Stem Applique

I found the above method especially awkward, actually impossible, when working with very narrow stems where the edges are trimmed so much that they begin to fray. So I developed another method, which I subsequently found on quilts dating from the 1930s. I'm sure that others have used this method, but I've never found it discussed in any book.

We are still working with the North Carolina Rose master pattern for this example. Cut out the fabric patch (Fig. 7–32A). The fabric will not be on a true bias, but will be flexible enough to work with. Lay the fabric, wrong side up, over the penciled stem line on the background block. The outer (bigger) curved line of the patch should lie over the outer curved line of the master (Fig. 7–34) where it joins the flower (Fig. 7–24). *Do not pin it to the background block.* Note how the fabric patch curves away from the master lines. Using

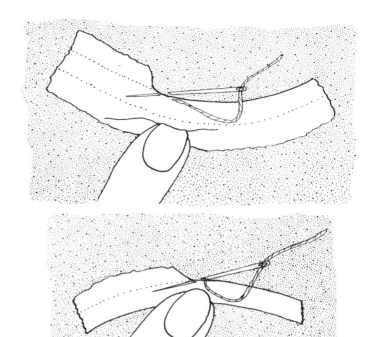

7–23 Always applique inside (concave) curves first. The dashed line indicates the stitching line of the master pattern on the background fabric.

7–24 Place the stem's large curve, wrong side up, over the large curve penciled onto the background block. The patch will curve away from the master line.

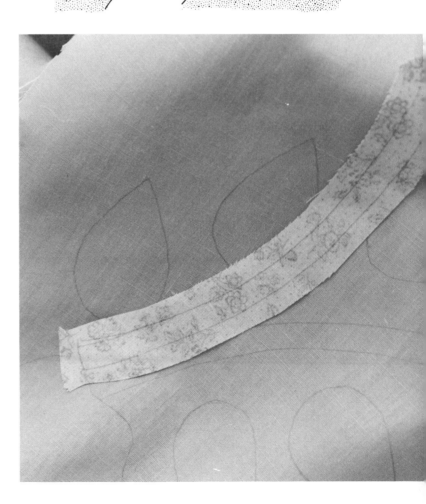

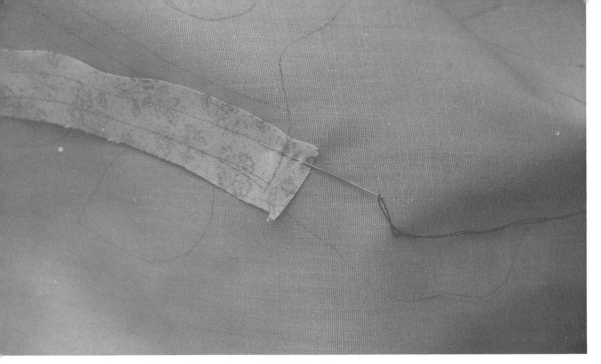

7–25   Start the running stitch in the flower area.

7–26   Shift the stem over to the penciled line only ⅓ inch ahead of where you are sewing.

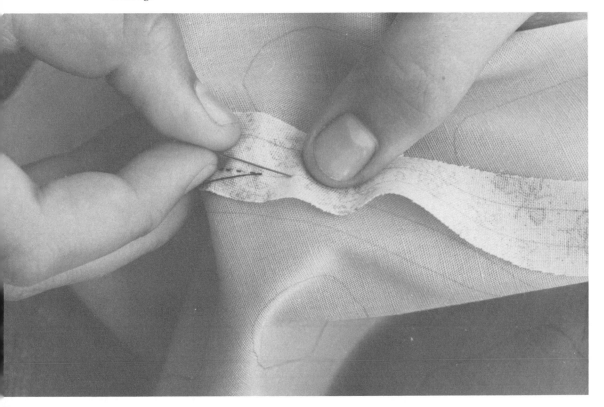

a single, knotted thread, sew the outer line of the patch to the outer line of the master with a tiny running stitch. Make sure that there is about a ¼-inch seam allowance at the top of the stem where it extends into the adjoining flower. See Fig. 7–24 for the placement.

Start the running stitch in the end seam allowance (Fig. 7–25). Take three or four stitches on the needle each time and then pull the thread through. Put the needle tip into the stem patch seam allowance about ⅓ inch ahead of the last stitch and shift the fabric over enough so that the two pencil lines align, one atop the other (Fig. 7–26). The pencil line will not be visible on the master, so fold the fabric stem back on itself to see if the needle has been placed accurately (Fig. 7–27). If so, pull the thread through. If not, remove the needle, reposition the fabric stem and sew again. Continue sewing the outer curve to the far end of the seam allowance. Knot the thread and cut, leaving a ¼-inch tail.

If you reach the far end of the strip and find that it is not long enough to extend into the flower area, you will have to pull it off and start over. What happened? The patch was marked using the template, so it had to be long enough to begin with—if you remembered to leave a ¼-inch seam allowance when cutting. The answer is in how the fabric was shifted with the needle. Instead of moving the fabric directly over to the master line, it was moved, however slightly, back toward the seam already sewn. This results in a very wavy stem when the final edge is sewn down (Fig. 7–28). It will take some practice to sew this seam properly, but by the time the fourth stem is sewn, you will be quite good at it.

If the seam allowance on the sewn edge is too wide, trim it now (Fig. 7–29). Next fold the stem fabric over so that the fabric is right side up. It should be smooth and flat. The inside curved edge is to be sewn using the applique technique discussed in Figs. 7–8 and 7–9. Trim the seam allowance, if necessary, as you sew. Each edge has been sewn using a different method, but the finished product should look smooth and neat.

CIRCLES

Unless a circle is quite large, say 3 inches in diameter, it is very difficult to make it really round, even following a master pattern. I finally decided not to use master patterns for circles, but to applique them in the following manner.

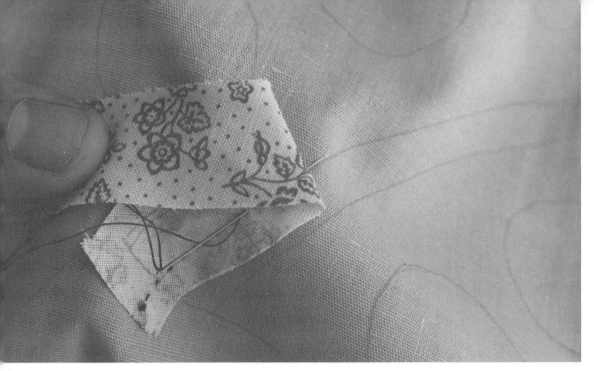

7–27 Fold the stem back on itself, with the needle still in place, to see if you are on the master line. If not, pull out the needle and restitch.

7–28 If the stem is rippled after the inside curve is sewn, the stem patch was shifted while this side was being appliqued. Undo and try again!

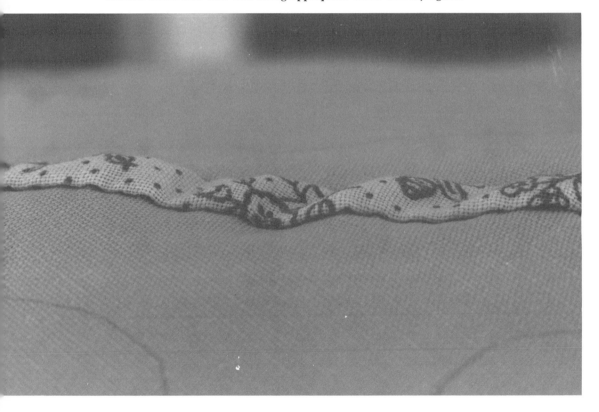

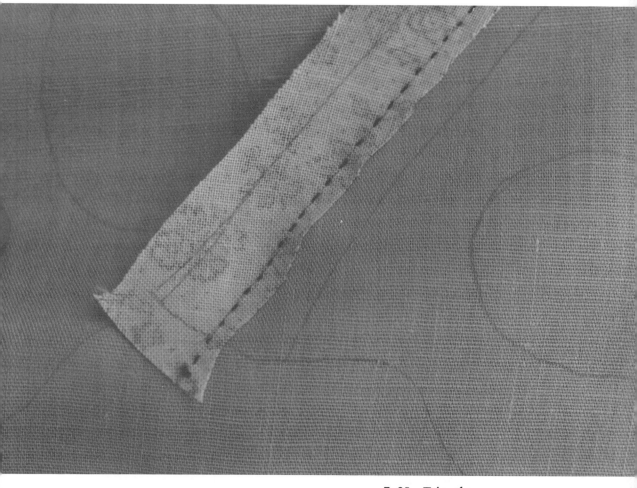

7–29   Trim the sewn seam
allowance to about ⅛ inch.

Using a pencil, trace around a circle template on the applique fabric. Cut the patch out on the penciled line (seam allowance is included). With a knotted, single thread, sew a tiny running stitch around the entire outer edge of the patch. The stitches should be as close to the edge as possible without fraying the material. Draw the thread up as tight as possible to gather the fabric. *Do not* cut the thread. The patch will look like a ball. Flatten the ball so that it forms a circle with the raw edges centered on the wrong side (Fig. 7–30). Position the circle in the desired area and applique down, using the same thread that gathered the circle. The applique stitches should be very close together (Fig. 7–31). If any little points have formed, take a stitch right into the point and it will disappear when the thread is pulled taut.

A circle can be stuffed, if you desire. Sew as directed above, but after sewing two-thirds of the circle, poke a little loose batting into the opening and then continue appliqueing. Don't stuff too tightly or the background fabric will pull out of shape.

It will probably take several tries to determine the correct size of the template, since so much of the fabric is drawn up to the back when gathering. To give you an indication, I used the end of a large spool of thread as a template for the flower center on the North Carolina Rose, and a dime for the Elizabethan Flower circles.

ELIZABETHAN FLOWER
Like North Carolina Rose, Elizabethan Flower is not beginner's applique; but I have my beginners learn with it. Applique will never be a problem for you, if you master both of these blocks. I would suggest doing the North Carolina Rose first, since it is easier (see color Fig. 3 and the cover).

Start by appliqueing the flower center (Fig. 7–33A). Only the top curved edge needs to be appliqued; attach the remaining two sides with a small running stitch. These edges will be covered by pattern pieces B and B1. The stem leaves are next. They are tiny and real doozies! Don't use a loosely woven fabric for them. (Refer to Points and Curves for directions.) Next, applique the flower stem and sides (33H, B, B1). It doesn't matter in what order the large leaves and petals are appliqued, since they are not attached to anything. The circles are done in the manner described above (Circles).

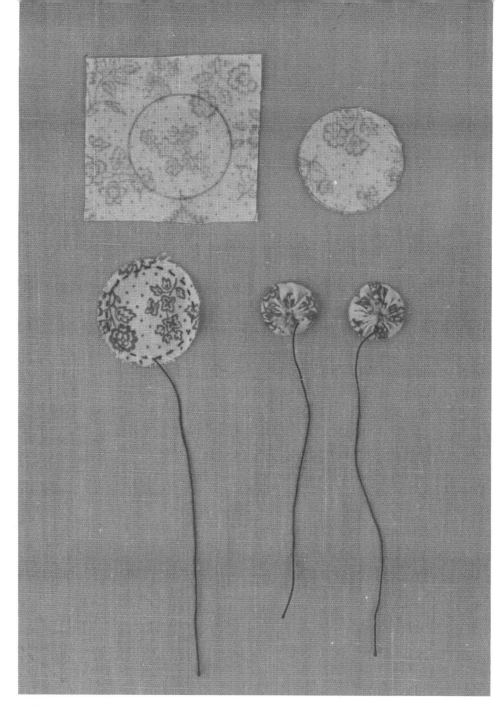

7–30 Making a circle. Trace a circle template (seams included) and cut the patch out on the pencil line. With a single, knotted thread, sew a tiny running stitch around the entire outer edge. Draw the thread up as tight as possible. Flatten the ball. Even the gathers with the needle tip.

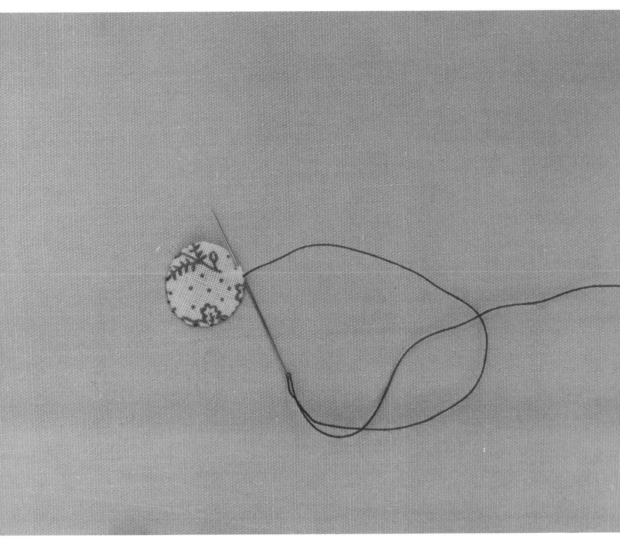

7–31 Use the same thread that gathered the circle, and stitch very close around the circle's edge to get a smooth curve. There may be small points around the circle. Take a stitch right into the point, and it will disappear when the thread is pulled taut.

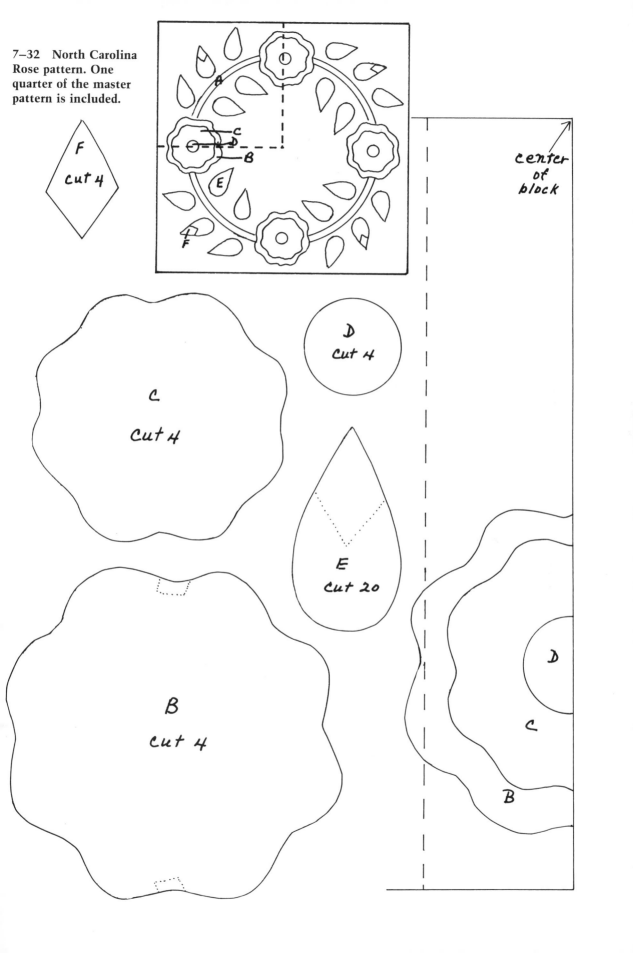

7–32 North Carolina Rose pattern. One quarter of the master pattern is included.

F
cut 4

center of block

D
Cut 4

C
Cut 4

E
Cut 20

B
cut 4

D

C

B

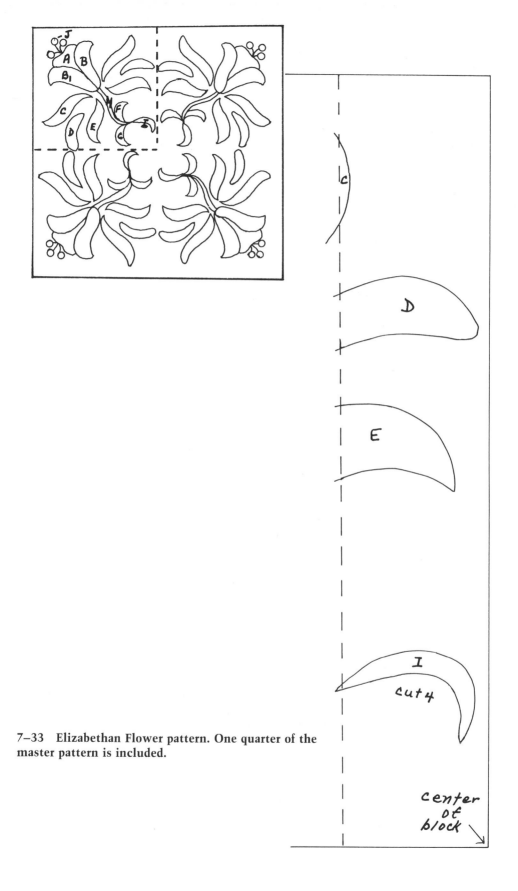

7–33 **Elizabethan Flower pattern. One quarter of the master pattern is included.**

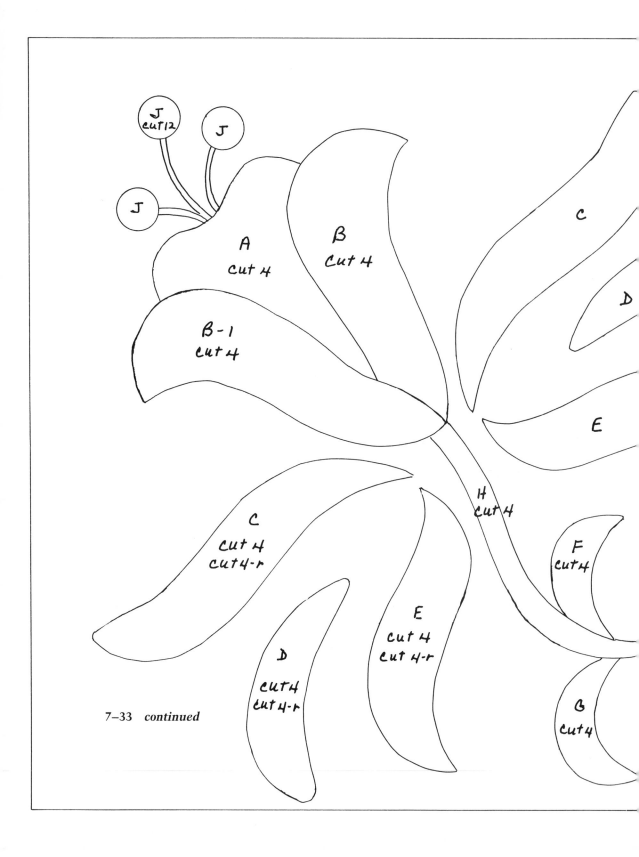

J cut12

J

J

A
cut 4

B
Cut 4

B-1
cut 4

C

D

E

H
cut 4

C
cut 4
cut4-r

F
cut4

E
cut 4
cut 4-r

D
cut4
cut 4-r

B
cut4

7–33   continued

Again, don't expect perfect results to begin with. Each stem and flower will look progressively better. I do recommend appliqueing all of one type patch before going on to the next. In that way, you get a lot of practice with a particular shape.

ADDITIONAL THOUGHTS ON APPLIQUE

The blocks covered in this chapter are not beginner's designs! They are advanced applique, taught with a completely new method. If you are like all my other students, you are now exhausted and very frustrated. And you've probably produced less than spectacular results. You are undoubtedly wondering why I chose these patterns and not something easier. After all you are a beginner—at least to the master pattern technique.

I could certainly show you how to applique an easy design like Sunbonnet Sue. That pattern has no really difficult points and only very gentle curves. But would I really be helping you? You need to learn how to do the difficult applique. I imagine you can figure out easy applique for yourself. As I tell my classroom students, "Yes, applique is hard. Yes, it does take time to learn, but once you have learned, you will find it easy and fun!"

Chapter Eight

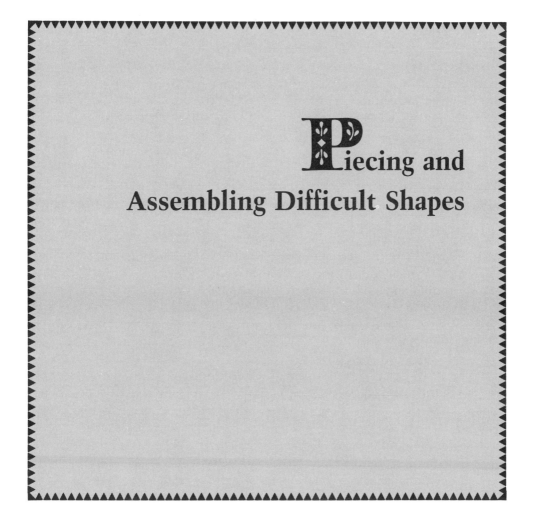

Piecing and
Assembling Difficult Shapes

As with all the piecing previously discussed, marking and sewing is exactly the same for curves and stars, but there are logistical problems resulting from the shapes of the patches. These particular problems will be covered in this chapter.

PIECING CURVES

No matter how gentle or sharp the curve, the trick is *not* to pin the entire seam allowance at the same time. In this instance, I will use the Starred Circle block (color Fig. 7) as an example. I developed this design to give extensive experience with curves, both gentle and acute. The more gentle curves will probably not present any problems, but do follow the directions given below. The piecing will be easier and the pieces will lie flat when completed.

Starred Circle Assembly

I am giving instructions for piecing the most acute curve in this block first. Follow these directions for piecing all curved units in Starred Circle. Pattern template E (Fig. 8–5) is a 180-degree curve, or a complete half circle, that fits into template D. Both of these templates are marked with slash lines. These lines should be placed on your working templates and then duplicated onto the fabric patches in the seam allowance area (Fig. 8–1). After marking the slash lines and cutting out patch D, clip halfway into the seam allowance on the concave edge every inch (Fig. 8–2). This allows the curved edge to be pulled into a fairly straight line. It is not necessary to clip patch E, but you may find it helpful to cut tiny V shapes from its convex edge to remove excess material that could wrinkle when pressed.

Pin only one-half of the seam allowance to begin with. Match the center markings and each successive mark, down to the point where you will start sewing (Fig. 8–3). *Note:* Patch D does not start at the exact bottom edge of patch E. Match the Xs on each patch or they will never fit together.

Start sewing the seam allowance, as usual. When working with curves, it will be more difficult to align the penciled stitching lines on both patches, but it is essential that you do so. You will probably find that only two or three stitches at a time can be taken on the needle (on a straight seam, four or five

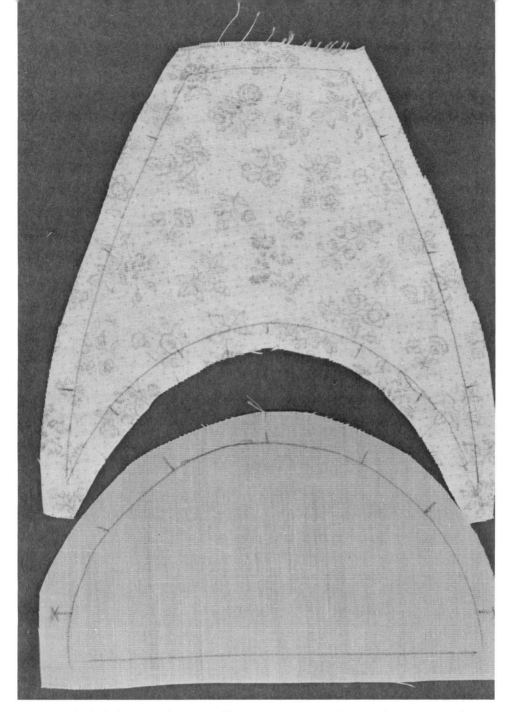

8–1 Mark slash lines in the seam allowances corresponding to the marks on the template patterns on patches D and E.

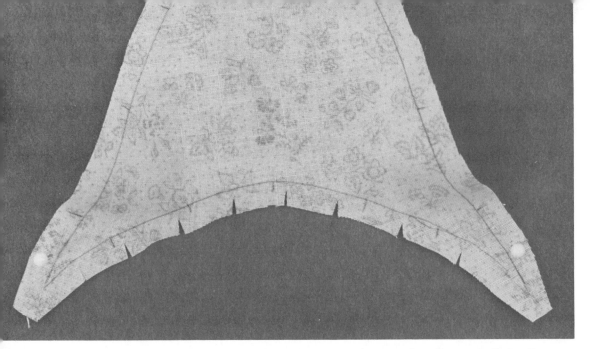

8–2   Clip the concave edge of patch D at 1-inch intervals. Clip one-half the distance to the stitching line.

8–3   Pin at the center mark and at the point at which you will start sewing (the X). Pin in between these two points. Sew from the X to the center mark.

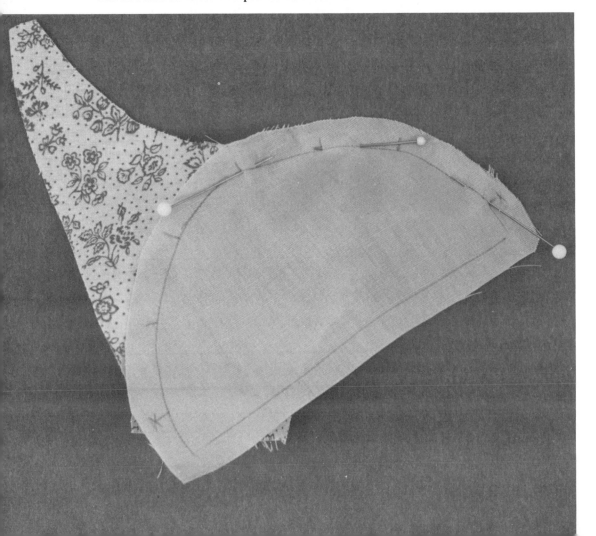

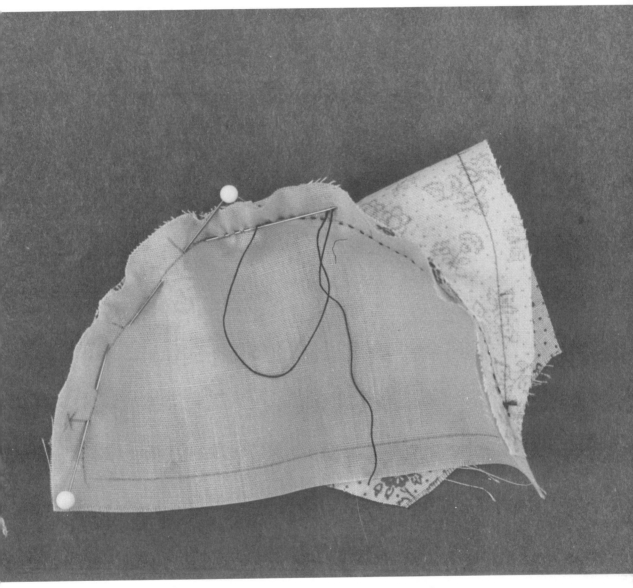

8–4   Pin the remaining X and slash marks and continue sewing the seam.

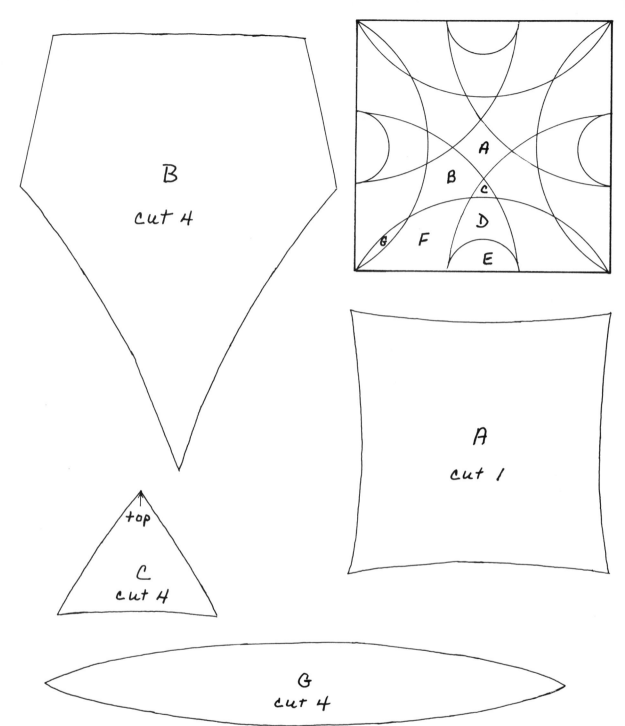

B

cut 4

A

cut 1

top

C
cut 4

G
cut 4

8–5 **Starred Circle pattern.**

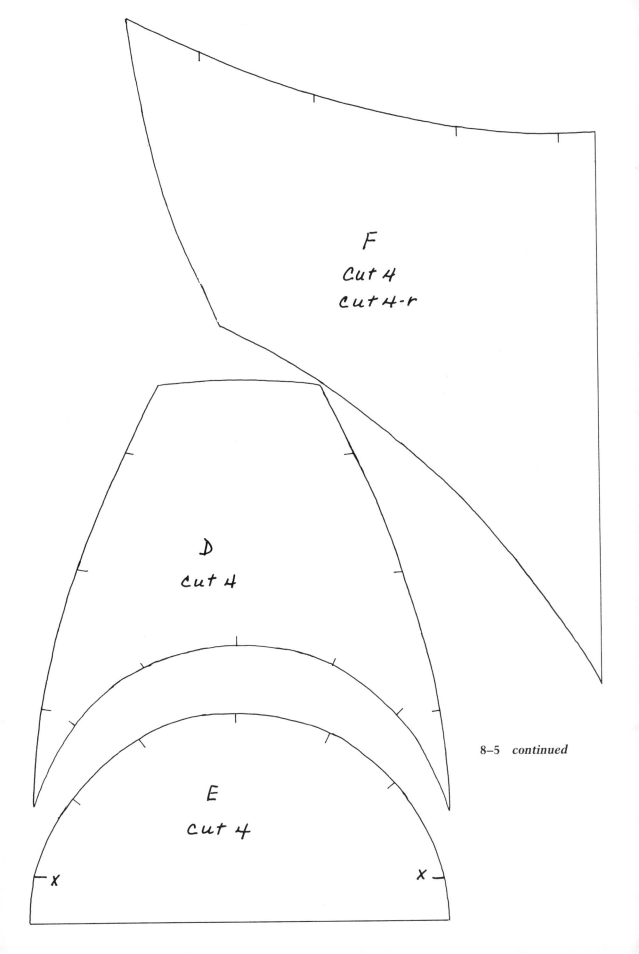

F

Cut 4
Cut 4-r

D

cut 4

E

cut 4

x   x

8–5   continued

can be taken). Once you have sewn up to the center pin, stop sewing and pin the remainder of the seam line, matching slash marks and the last X. Finish sewing the seam line (Fig. 8–4).

This block is joined in units and assembled from the center out (Fig. 8–6). Patch B has one patch C joined to each of its short edges. Repeat this for another patch B. Now piece the center patch A to the two remaining B patches. Join the two units, C-B-C, on either side of unit B-A-B. The entire center is now pieced. Press all the seam to the outside edges.

Join patches D to E as described at the beginning of this chapter, if you have not already done so. Piece an F patch to each side of D-E. Next, piece two of these units on opposite sides of the completed center. Piece a G patch to each side of the two remaining F-D-E-F units. Join these to the last two sides of the block for the completed design.

Premarking Your Own Curved Templates

On each of the template patterns in Starred Circle, slash lines have been given for matching to a corresponding slash mark. If you are working with another pattern, you will have to make your own. Take the two working templates that must be joined and fit them together. Mark slash lines from one template to the other at the height of the curve (center) and in as many places as you think necessary. Transfer these lines to the fabric patches when marking, prior to cutting. It doesn't matter if the slash marks do not divide the curve exactly. What is important is to join the concave and convex curves at the corresponding markings. Proceed with pinning and sewing as detailed above.

PIECING STARS

Any time six or more patches are joined together, you are working with the fundamentals of joining a star center, even though the finished design may not form a full star. Each quilter has his or her own opinion on how best to piece a star and have an accurate center joining. I believe the majority join an eight-pointed star first in units of two, then four and finally the two sets of four together with a straight seam to form the full star (Fig. 8–7). I have trouble

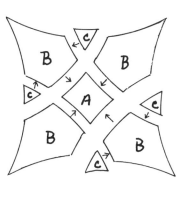

step 1

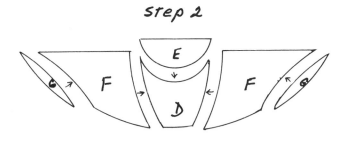

step 2

piece 2 units

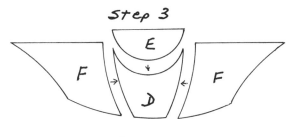

step 3

piece 2 units

step 4

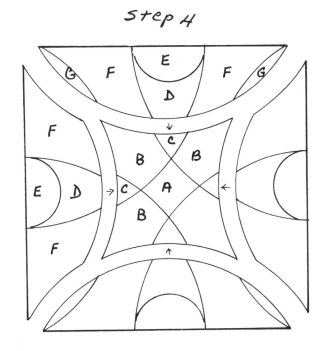

8–6 Assembly of Starred Circle.

Piecing and Assembling Difficult Shapes | 139

with this method. Slight shifting seems to result, at least for me, and the center isn't always perfect. When piecing a twelve-pointed star this problem is really magnified. I have found the following method very easy for beginners and extremely accurate. We will work with the Broken Crystals block (see color Fig. 3).

Broken Crystals Assembly

You will notice that the edges of the templates are marked with varying numbers of slash marks (Fig. 8–14). These do not have to be sewn slash to slash as with the curved patches in Starred Circle. They simply indicate which patch edge joins to its neighbor patch. For instance, the single slash on patch A joins to the edge of patch D that has a single slash.

To piece the center, pin patch A to patch B and sew the seam from the center point to the outer edge. This is important since shifting of even a single thread or two at the point would throw the center matching off. It is not as crucial at the outer edge. Again, careful marking, pinning and sewing are mandatory for accuracy.

Continue adding A and B patches alternately until all patches are sewn into a single row (Fig. 8–8). Close the star by sewing the end patches A and

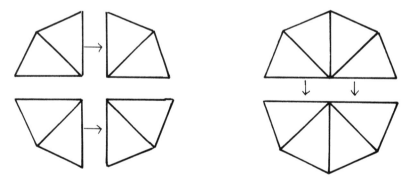

8–7 The method generally used for piecing a star. The unit is joined in quarters, then halves, and finally into a completed block.

8–8 The preferred method to make a star is by joining patches in a single row.

B together. This method of joining will leave a small hole in the very center of the star (Fig. 8–9). If the hole is large enough for you to stick your finger through, something went wrong. Was the template marking really accurate at the points? Did you sew on the pencil lines or go off a bit? Did you sew from the center of the star to the outside edges? Decide where you went wrong, rip out and make the necessary corrections.

Closing the Center Hole

The hole must now be closed. Be sure to use a single, knotted thread that best matches the fabrics. Bring the needle up through the fabric from the under side of the block into one patch at the edge of the hole (Fig. 8–10). All remaining stitching will be done from the *right* side of the block. Take a tiny stitch into the very point of each one of the patches at the hole's edge (Fig. 8–11). When all patches have been so stitched, pull the thread taut (Fig. 8–12). The hole should close with the center matching very accurately. If it is slightly off, take a few tiny stitches across the center to draw the unaligned points together (Fig. 8–13). When pulled taut, these stitches should not be visible. Take the needle to the back of the block, knot and then cut the thread. A perfect center!

The remainder of the block is assembled as in Fig. 8–15. Join patches D and E together; then add patch C. There will be a total of eight of these units. Piece unit D-E-C to each side of A-B by joining D to A and C to B. Remember, templates C, D and E have to be cut with four of the patches reversed. This is done by turning the template over. Next sew F to the two E's by flopping (See Chapter 5: Joining Multiple Edges [Flopping]). Sew patch G into each corner at the C's by flopping. Press.

Star Flower Assembly

Star Flower (color Fig. 3) is a pieced design that is to be appliqued to a background block as Grandmother's Flower Garden was. When cutting the center circle, it is imperative that you mark slash lines on the fabric patch for proper placement of the B and C patches. There are several ways to piece this block (Fig. 8–16), but the easiest is to piece two strips, each made by alternating four patches of B and C. Carefully pin one strip to the circle, matching the

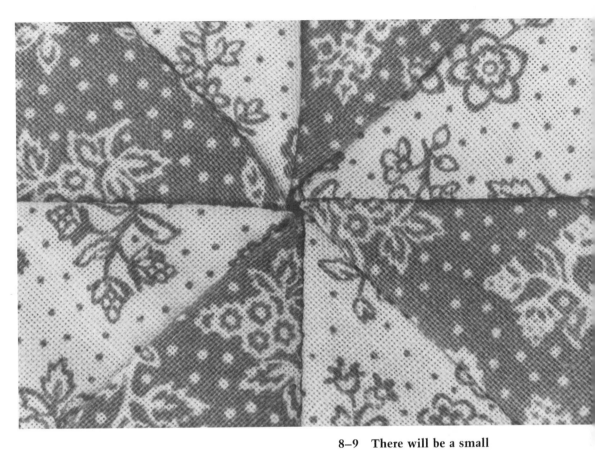

8–9   There will be a small hole at the very center of the star when the final seam is sewn. If the hole is so large you can put your finger through it, something went wrong in marking or piecing. Try again!

8–10   The hole must be closed. Bring the needle up from the back of the block into the edge of the hole.

8–11   Take a tiny stitch into the very point of each patch at the hole's edge. Do this in order.

8–12 Pull the thread taut. The hole will close very tightly.

8–13 If the patch points do not align, take a few stitches across the center to pull the points together. Take the thread to the back of the block, knot and cut.

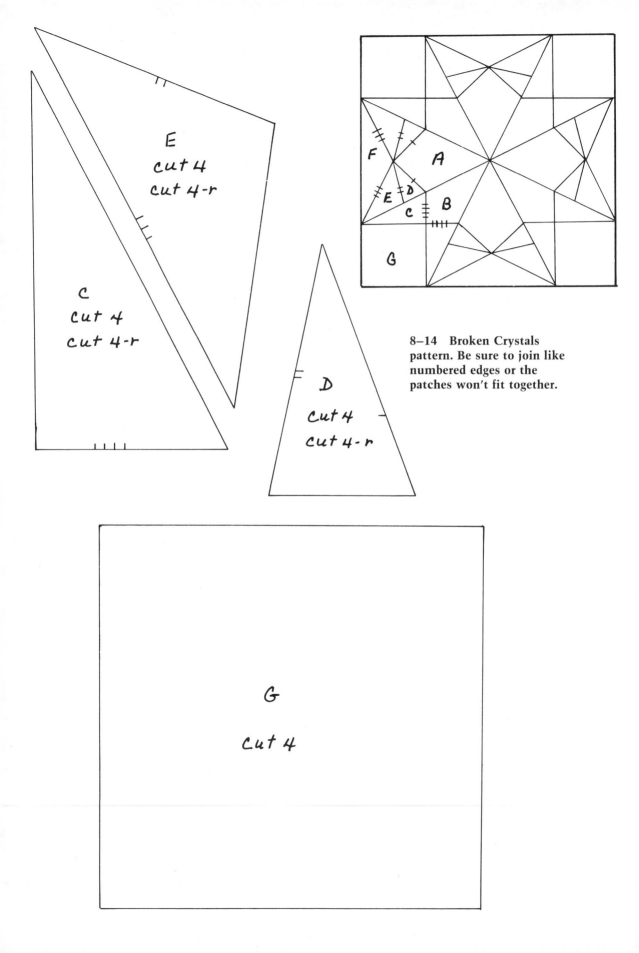

E
cut 4
cut 4-r

C
cut 4
cut 4-r

D
cut 4
cut 4-r

F

A

E

D

c

B

G

8–14 Broken Crystals pattern. Be sure to join like numbered edges or the patches won't fit together.

G
cut 4

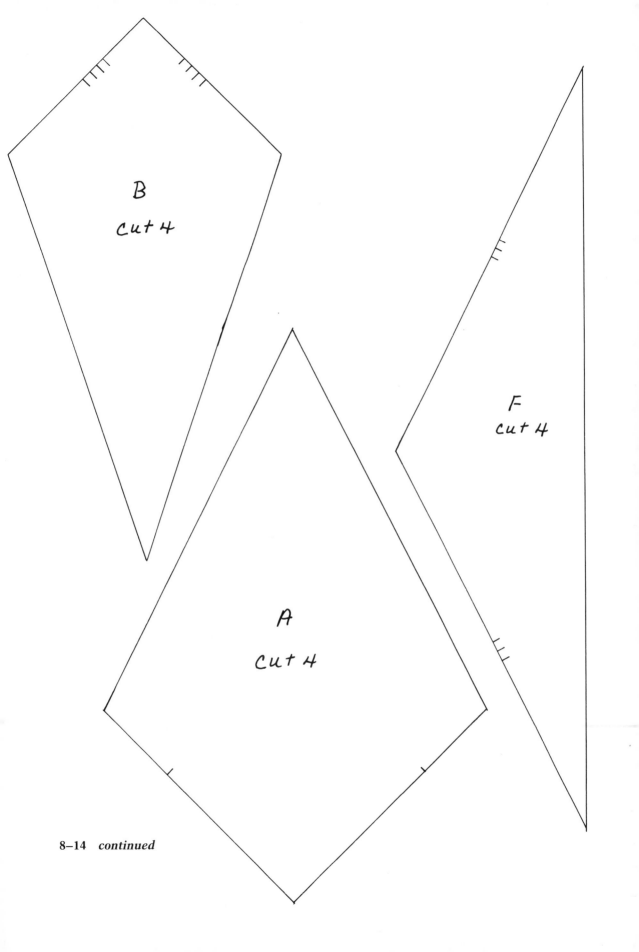

B
cut 4

F
cut 4

A
cut 4

8–14 *continued*

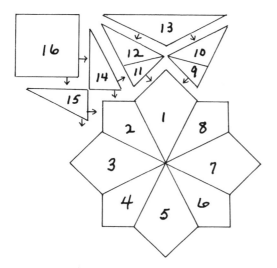

8–15 Broken Crystals assembly.

slash marks to the joining seams at B and C. Sew the strip to the circle, being certain that you don't stretch the fabric. Repeat for the other strip of B-C patches. Sew the two remaining open seams to join the star into a completed circle. Press. Baste the raw edges under as directed in Chapter 5: Basting. Center and pin the Star onto the background block. Applique in place.

Birds in Heaven Assembly

This block is also one of my designs (color Fig. 3). At first glance, it does not appear to present any special problems, but look more closely at the patterns (Fig. 8–18). Except for the four corner squares, it is comprised of triangles each of which appear to have at least two equal sides. Wrong. None of the triangle sides are of the same length, so great care must be taken to match the proper patch sides together. Again, make use of the slash marks on the template patterns as you did for Broken Crystals.

Follow the assembly in Fig. 8–19 very closely. Join patch A to patch B on slash line 1, eight times. Join these A-B units into a star center as detailed in Figs. 8–8 to 8–12. Join two patch C's together on slash line 2. Repeat three

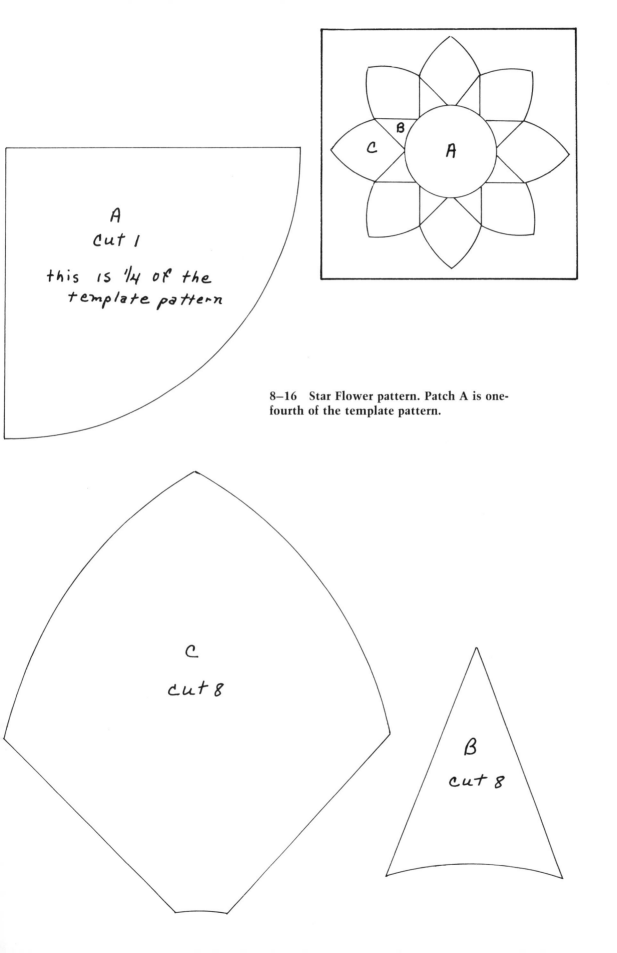

A
cut 1

this is ¼ of the
template pattern

B

C

A

8–16 Star Flower pattern. Patch A is one-
fourth of the template pattern.

C

cut 8

B

cut 8

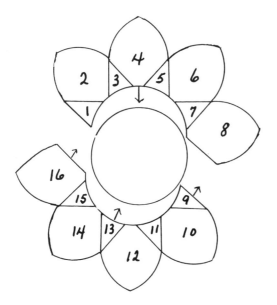

more times. Join each double C unit to two B's on slash line 3 by flopping. Piece a long unit of E-F-D-D-F-E, making sure that the correct slash lines are matched. Repeat three times more. Piece each of these long units to the 7 slash sides of two C's. Flop at the center point of the seam line. Piece a G patch into each corner by flopping. Press each separate unit as you piece and, finally, the completed block.

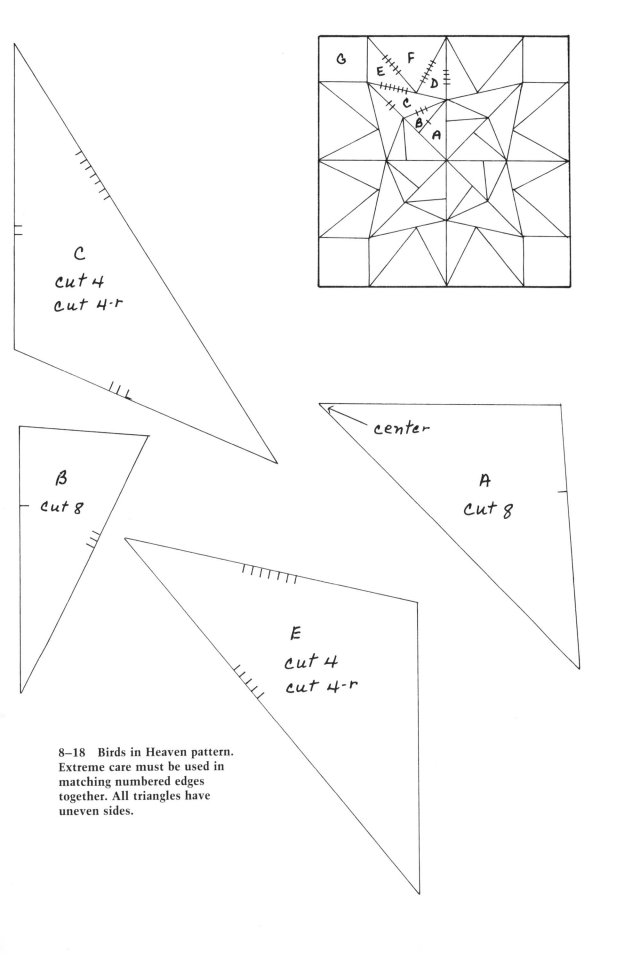

G

E F
D

C

B A

C
cut 4
cut 4·r

center

A
cut 8

B
cut 8

E
cut 4
cut 4·r

**8–18 Birds in Heaven pattern.
Extreme care must be used in
matching numbered edges
together. All triangles have
uneven sides.**

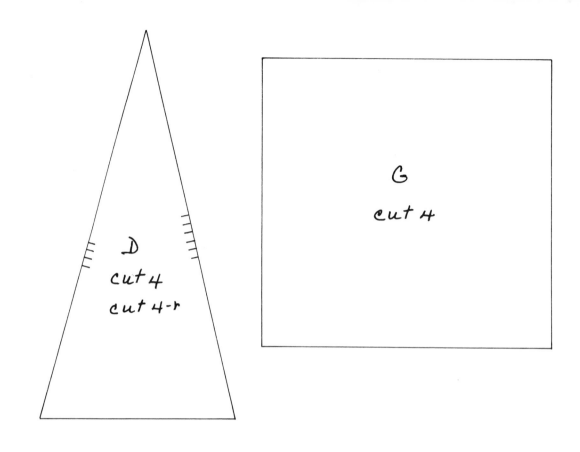

D

cut 4

cut 4-r

G

cut 4

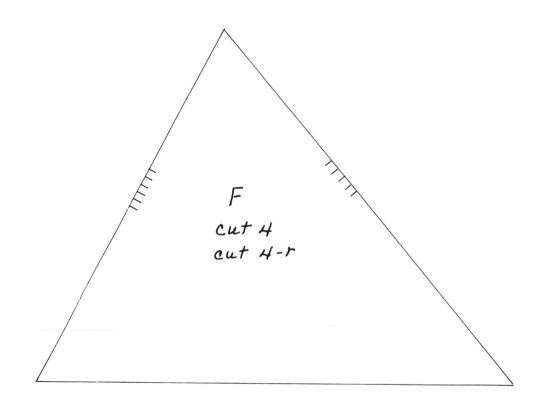

F

cut 4

cut 4-r

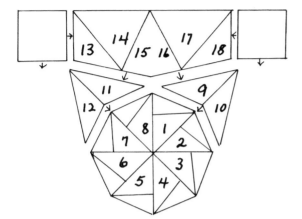

8–19   Birds in Heaven assembly.

Chapter Nine

Strip Assembly

All the techniques for piecing and applique have been discussed thoroughly. After you have constructed all the blocks needed for the quilt, you are ready to set them together with the sashing that has been marked and cut (see Chapter 4). Lay all the blocks on the floor and arrange them so that you are pleased with the balance. The blocks should be placed so that the colors and patterns are evenly distributed. For instance, if you have two blocks that are appliqued and contain a lot of red, don't put them next to each other. There are some pleasing arrangements shown in the color plates. Please realize, however, that no single arrangement is necessarily right; your choice should be dictated by both design and color use. Once you have decided on the placement, make a notation of it on your quilt layout, so you can refer to it later when setting the blocks.

MARKING QUILTING PATTERNS

Before the strip is basted together, it must be marked for the quilting pattern you intend to use. A pieced block, such as Birds in Heaven, can be outline quilted ¼ to ⅓ inch inside the seams. Outline quilting is marked *after* the strip has been basted together, set in the frame and you are actually quilting that area.

A second quilting method follows an appliqued design. The lines are marked, freehand, after the strip has been basted and set in the frame. It is almost the same as with the pieced block, but instead of following a geometric shape and using a ruler as a guide, you follow a free-form design and do the marking without a ruler. These lines are placed the same distance from the appliqued design as the outline quilting lines are from the seams, i.e., ¼ to ⅓ inch from the applique edge.

A third quilting method is a free-form, fancy pattern in either blocks, sashing or borders. It does not have to follow a pieced or appliqued shape already in the block. The pattern must be put on the fabric *before* the strip is basted together. For sashing and borders, I would do this before they are sewn to the blocks. The design is handled and applied as a master pattern (see Chapter 7, Master Pattern Applique).

A fourth method can be produced by using a moveable template. The shape is usually fairly simple, for it must be cut out with scissors from Mylar or a manila folder. Again, the strip should be in the frame and ready to quilt. After placing the template on the surface of the material, use a sharp pencil to trace the design onto the fabric. You can make your own quilt template, or you can purchase machine-made stencils. The ready-made stencils are usually fairly expensive, however, and may not be very accurate. If you are going to use an elaborate quilting design, I would recommend that the master pattern technique be used, both from the standpoint of accuracy and cost.

For the sampler quilt used as the example project, you will be using all four quilting methods. Fancy designs will be used in the borders, sashing, and the open areas of blocks such as Grandmother's Flower Garden and North Carolina Rose (see color Fig. 3). The designs in this chapter, Figs. 9–6 to 9–8, will give you some idea of what can be done. Make master patterns from these designs.

SETTING BLOCKS TO SASHING

Piecing sashing to blocks is done exactly the same as joining small patches, except that you are constructing larger units. You do have to be careful that the sash is pinned in evenly. Match the corner pencil lines and, using your finger, crease the center of the sash on its longest edge. Pin this crease mark to the seam line at the center of the block. Then pin each corner and any additional locations necessary to hold it securely (Fig. 9–1). Sew as usual. Remember, *do not* sew into the seam allowances.

Twin to Floor Strip Units

For the twin to the floor layout, you will have strip 1, with three blocks, each separated by a sash. Strip 2 has three blocks, each separated by a sash, plus the long center sash down one edge. There will be four border units, each comprised of the inner border and outer border. This makes a total of six strip units that have to be quilted and then joined together to make the quilt (Fig. 9–2).

CUTTING THE BATT AND BACKING

The backing fabric and batt must now be cut for each of the strips in Fig. 9–2. Use the completed top strips as patterns. Lay strip 1 on the backing fabric and cut around its raw edges. Do the same thing for the batt, making sure that

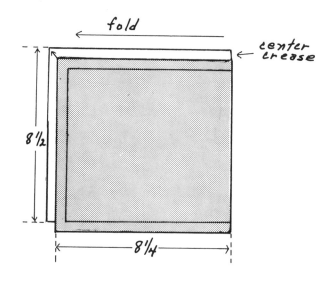

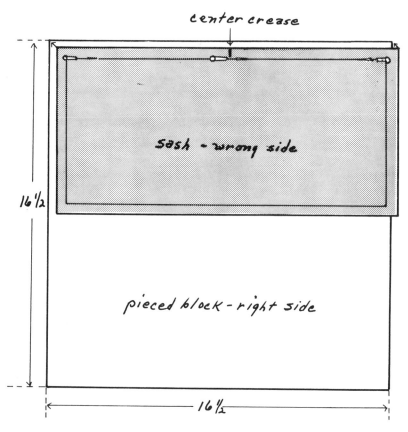

9–1 Find the sash center and pin it to the center of the block's edge. Any long units should be creased and pinned in this manner to insure accurate piecing. Always pin on the pencil lines.

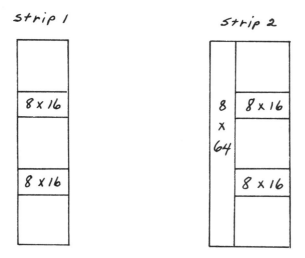

strip 1

strip 2

8 x 16

8 x 16

8
x
64

8 x 16

8 x 16

strips 3 - 6

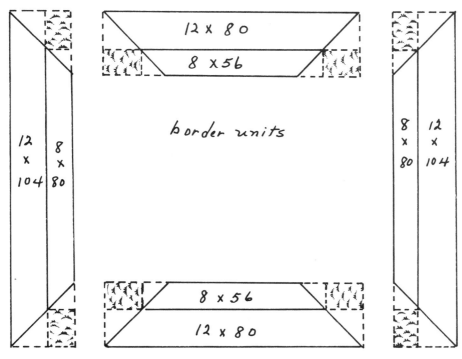

12 x 80

8 x 56

border units

12
x
104

8
x
80

8
x
80

12
x
104

8 x 56

12 x 80

9–2 Completed top strips for twin to floor quilt. Strips 1 and 2 are the blocks and sashing. Strips 3 through 6 are the borders. The patterned areas indicate fabric extensions to square off the strip ends.

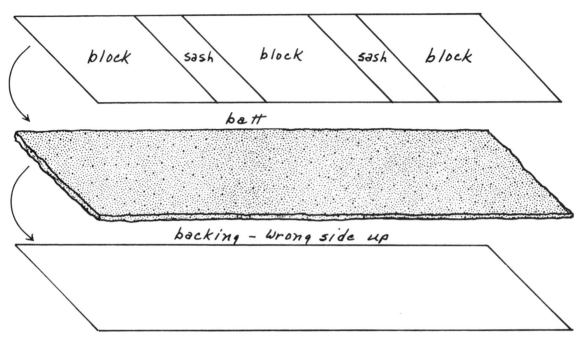

pieced strip - right side up

block   sash   block   sash   block

batt

backing - wrong side up

9–3 Assembling the backing, batt and top. Make sure all loose threads have been trimmed away and wrinkles pressed out.

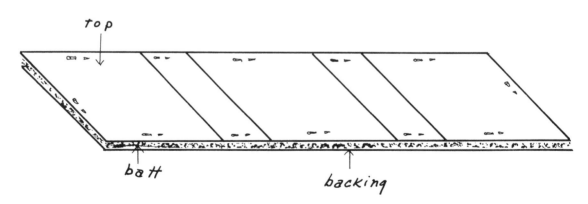

top

batt

backing

9–4 The strip is pinned together and ready for basting.

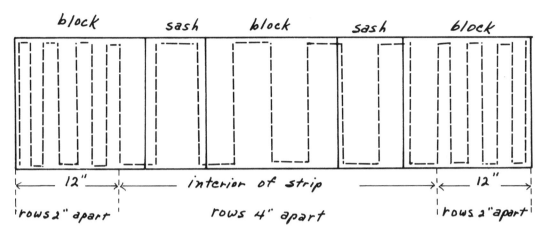

9–5 Top view of the strip basted together. The basting rows must be no more than 2 inches apart for a distance of 12 inches at each end of the strip; otherwise, you will have difficulty when quilting that area.

the batt has first been separated into a single layer. (Some batts tend to stick together after being packaged for a period of time.) Repeat this cutting process for each of the strips in Fig. 9–2. Because you have cut around the outer edges of the strips, the seam allowances have automatically been included in the backing and batt.

All of the backing strips can be cut down the length of the fabric as in cutting method 1 (see Chapter 4). You will use 41 inches of the 44-inch wide material. For some quilts, cutting method 2 might be the most economical. Again, you would piece the fabric where necessary and treat the seam as if it didn't exist.

STRIP ASSEMBLY

Place the backing strip, wrong side up, on a table. Place the batt strip on top of it. Smooth out any wrinkles in the batt. Carefully lay the top strip on the batt, right side up (Fig. 9–3). Make sure that any loose threads have been

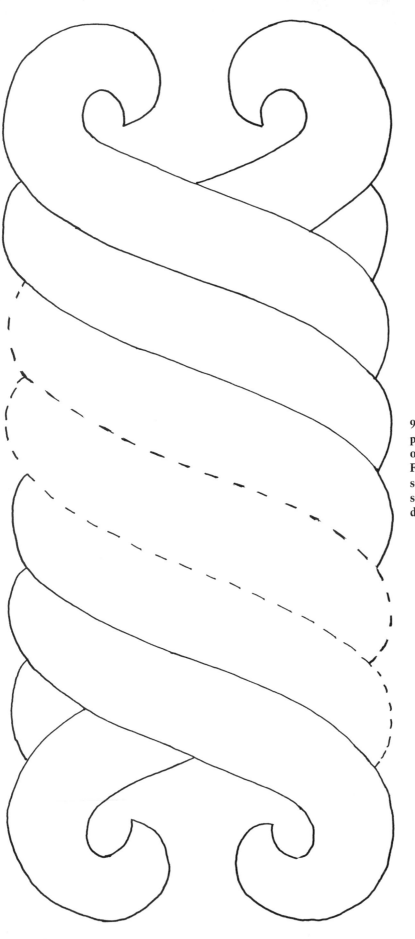

9–6 Sashing quilting pattern that was used on my quilt in color Fig. 3. Add enough segments to make the sash 15 inches or the desired length.

B

A

miter line

9–7 The inner- and outer-border quilting pattern for the quilt in Color Fig. 3. Make a master and match the broken lines and letters for the full pattern. Add enough plumes to make it long enough to fit the border of your quilt.

D

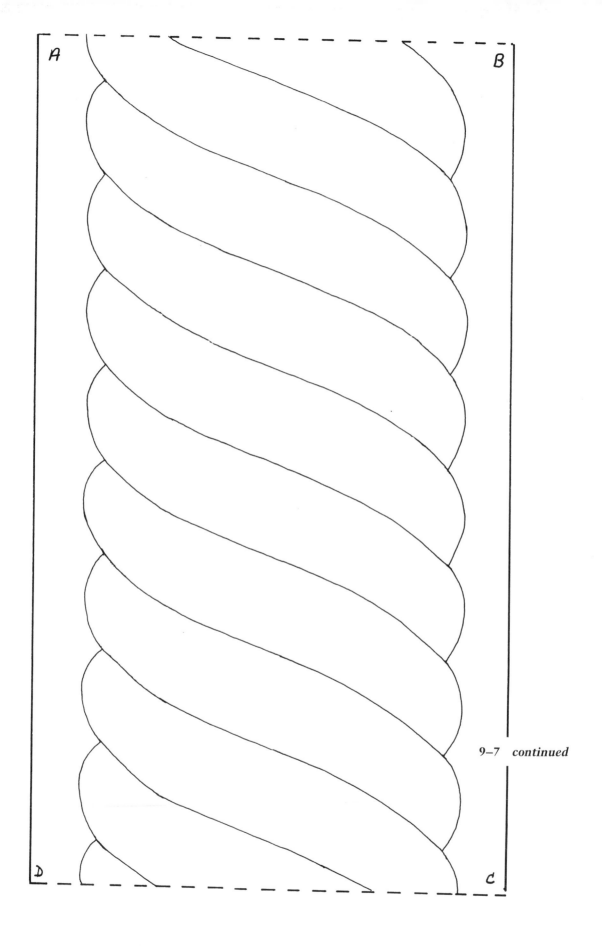

9-7 continued

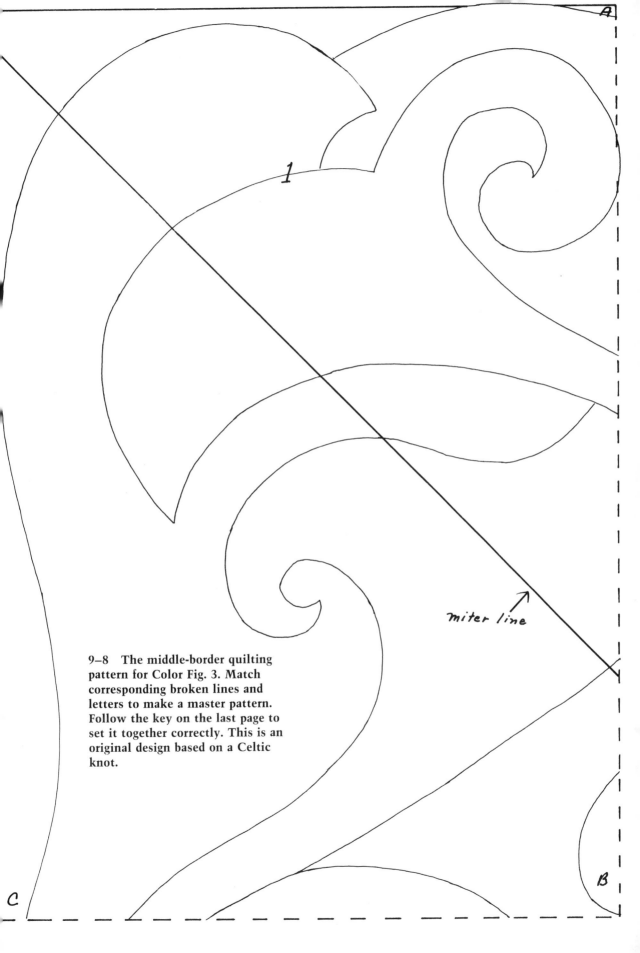

A

1

miter line

9–8   The middle-border quilting
pattern for Color Fig. 3. Match
corresponding broken lines and
letters to make a master pattern.
Follow the key on the last page to
set it together correctly. This is an
original design based on a Celtic
knot.

C

B

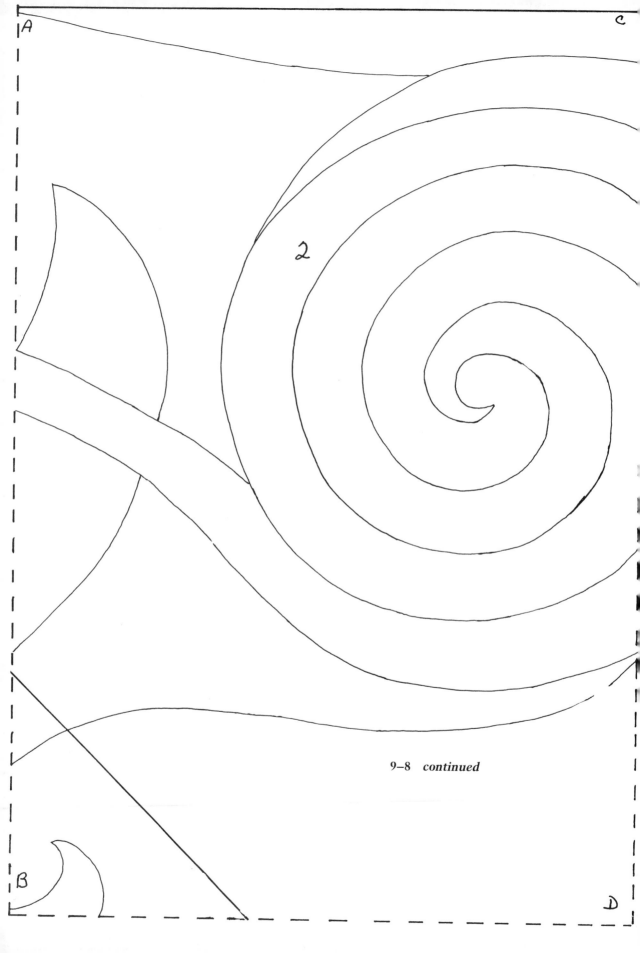

A

C

2

9–8 *continued*

B

D

C

E

3

9–8   *continued*

D

F

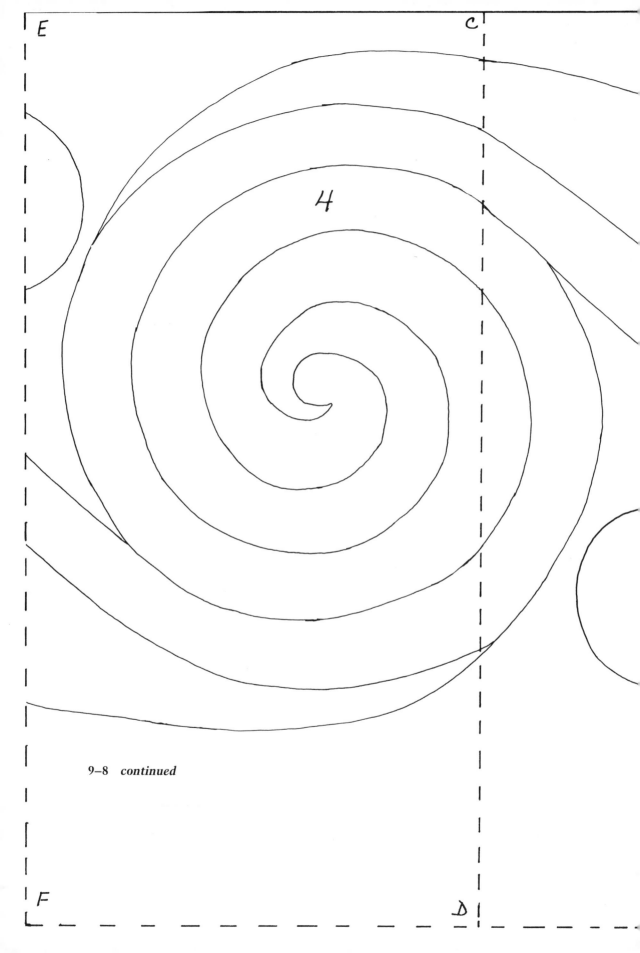

E

c

4

9–8 continued

F

D

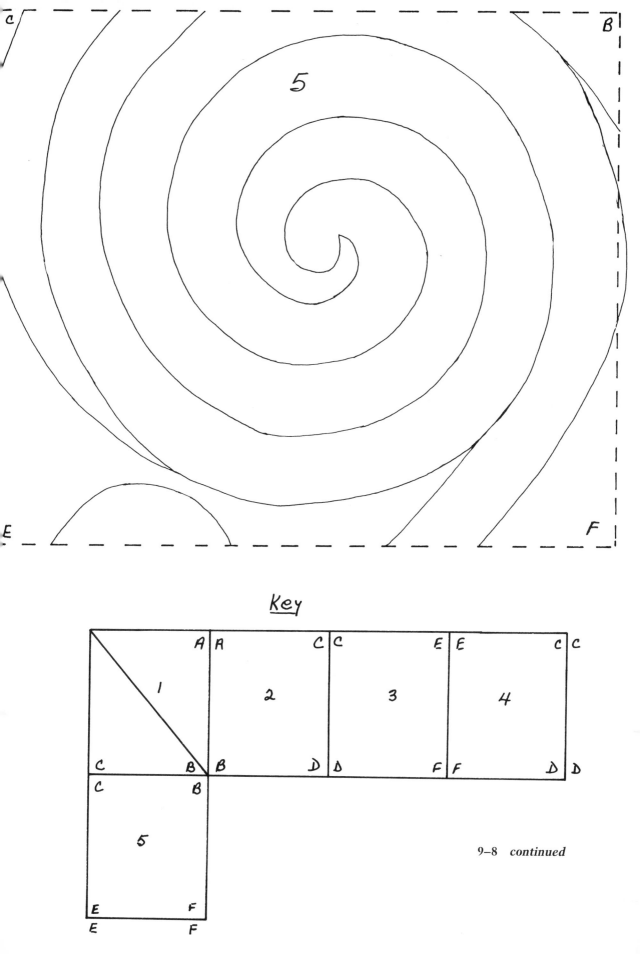

5

C

B

E

F

Key

A	A C	C E	E C
1	2	3	4
C B	B D	D F	F D

C B

5

E F

9–8 *continued*

trimmed from the seams of the strip. Pin the three units (backing, batt and top) together at the outer edges (Fig. 9–4).

The strip must be basted together through all three layers. Use a "sharp" or embroidery needle and a long thread. Basting thread works well and is certainly cheaper than #50 thread. In any case, use only white thread; colored thread can leave dots of color in the fabric when it's removed.

The basting stitches can be about 2 inches long. The basting rows should be 2 inches apart and 12 inches in from each end of the strip. In the middle area of the strip, the rows can be 4 inches apart. Work the basting rows up the strip in a serpentine fashion. This method will hold the strip securely (Fig. 9–5).

Chapter Ten

Quilting As You Go

The strip is now ready to be pinned into the quilt-as-you-go frame. A major advantage in this type of quilt making is that you can be quilting on a strip while you are still piecing blocks for it. This not only seems to speed up the process, but it keeps you from being bored by having to do all of one phase before going on to the next.

The frame you use can be a purchased needlepoint frame or one that has been made by following the directions in Chapter 1. I have frames in varying lengths from 12 inches, for borders or small pillows, to 36 inches, a really cumbersome size. The most versatile, easily handled frame length is 24 inches. This length will allow you to quilt a 16-inch block with an attached 5- or 6-inch wide sashing.

ATTACHING THE STRIP TO THE FRAME

Place the shortest edge of the basted strip, top up, along the edge of the tape. The loose edge of the tape should be toward the center of the frame (see Fig. 1–2e). Make sure that the strip is centered on the tape. Pin the seam allowance of the strip to the edge of the tape about every 2 inches (Fig. 10–1). Do not pin too close to the dowel or you may quilt the tape to the strip (Fig. 10–2). *Note:* If you live in an area of high humidity, do not use pins. Baste the strip to the tape with white thread to prevent rust spots. Also, protect the tack heads or staples used to attach the tape to the dowel by painting them with clear nail polish. Let the polish dry thoroughly before using the frame.

It is easiest to pin or baste one end of the strip into the frame, roll half the strip around the dowel, then pin the opposite end of the strip to the other tape and roll that end.

When rolling the strip onto the dowel, you must take care to roll the basted unit as one piece. Even though it has been basted, it can shift easily. Don't tug on the strip as it is rolled. Grasp the fabric strip gently, but firmly, making sure it goes around the dowel as a single unit. Each dowel should be rotated to the outside of the frame so that the basted unit lies above the dowels (see Fig. 1–2e).

As you roll the strip onto the dowel, the backing will be going around a smaller circumference than the top because of the batt's thickness. Therefore, the backing will wrinkle as the strip is rolled on (Fig. 10–3). Don't worry about

10–1   Pinning the strip into the quilt-as-you-go frame. If you live in an area of high humidity, baste the strip instead of pinning.

10–2   Back view of the tape. Pin or baste close to the edge of the tape.

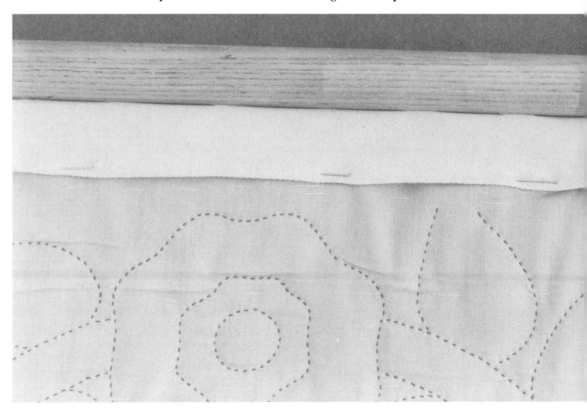

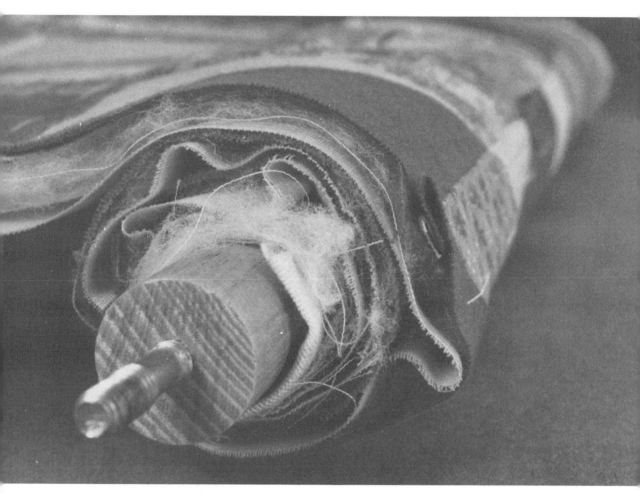

10–3 End view of the
basted unit that has been
rolled onto the frame. The
end bar has been removed.
Notice the wrinkling of the
strip.

it. When that area is rolled to the center of the frame for quilting, the backing will straighten out. *Note:* The strip should be rolled taut for quilting; but if you are using the running stitch, it may be easier to quilt if the strip is loosened slightly.

QUILTING

There are two ways to do the quilting stitch. Most people are familiar with the running stitch. I prefer the less well-known "punch and poke" stitch. I'll discuss both methods in detail, and you can choose the best technique for you. I would urge you to give the "punch and poke" stitch a good try. It takes longer to perfect, but gives better results on the back of the quilt, where quality shows. A good quilter will usually glance at the surface of a quilt and quickly flip up a corner to see what the stitches look like on the back. There hangs the tale!

The Running Stitch

Most quilters use the running stitch. The right hand holds the needle at an angle and inserts it into the quilt from the top until the tip comes out the back (Fig. 10–4). The left hand stays under the surface of the quilt and "feels" for the needle tip to come through (Fig. 10–5). The tip is then pushed back up to return out the surface of the quilt. You can take from one to three, four or five stitches on the needle. The eye end of the needle is pushed by the middle finger of the right hand until the needle can be grasped and pulled through. This is really the same stitch that was used for piecing, only now the needle is going through three thicknesses. Left-handed quilters would hold the needle in the left hand and have the right hand under the quilt.

"Punch and Poke" Stitch

To do the "punch and poke" stitch, one hand (either one) holds the threaded needle absolutely perpendicular to the fabric, while the index finger "punches" the needle straight down through all three layers (Fig. 10–6). The other hand is underneath the frame; the fingers form a triangle and apply

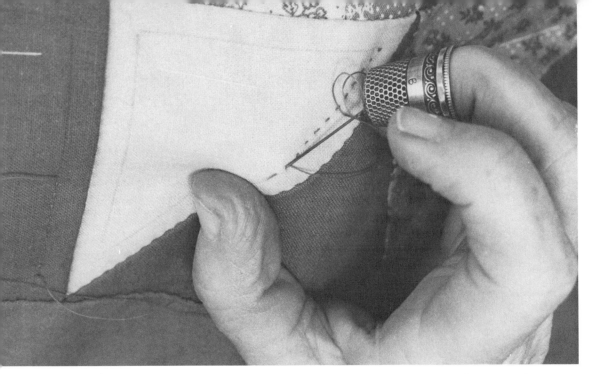

10–4 Top view of a right-handed quilter doing the running stitch. Notice the "hills" being created by pressure from the hand under the quilt.

10–5 Left index finger feeling the needle point from the underside of the quilt. Some quilters cover this finger with a strip of adhesive tape to prevent pricking.

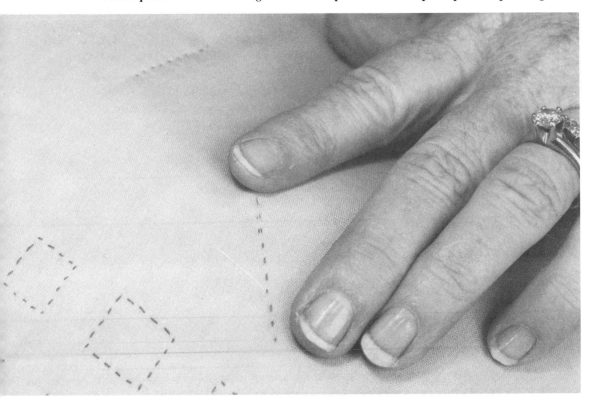

upward pressure on the fabric where the needle will come through (Fig. 10–7). This creates a slight bulge and smooths out the backing. The hand under the frame grasps the needle tip as it emerges out the backing and pulls the needle completely through, but only far enough to turn the needle around and poke it back up to the surface (Fig. 10–8). Usually this means that no more than 2 inches of thread are pulled through to the back. The hand on top then brings the needle out and pulls the thread taut (Fig. 10–9). In essence, each stitch is an individual one.

It is extremely important to remember that one hand always works from the top of the frame and one hand from underneath. The hand on the top *does not* move under the frame to pull the needle through to the back. That would be self-defeating for developing rhythm and speed.

Quilting Thread Tension

You may make very neat quilting stitches, but if the thread tension is not correct, your quilting will not look sharp. If your thread is too tight, the fabric will be puckered. To correct this, do not pull on the thread quite as much when drawing the length through the quilt.

It's not as easy to see if your stitches are too loose. To check the tension, slip the needle under a stitch and pull up. If a loop of thread can be drawn up, the tension is too loose. Pull the thread more taut when quilting.

There should be a happy medium in your thread tension. You want the three layers to be held together firmly, but not so firmly that the quilt puckers. When the quilt is washed, the quilt thread will probably shrink a little and you will notice some puckering. This is part of the beauty of the quilt, but it should not be confused with quilting stitches that are so tight that they pull the quilt out of shape.

Thimbles

Many women have been taught that they have to use a thimble to be a good seamstress. If you work best with a thimble, terrific! But if you are one of the fifty percent of women who do not use thimbles, don't feel guilty about

10–6   "Punching" the needle through to the back of the quilt. Notice that the needle is at an absolute right angle to the fabric.

10–7   Fingers, forming a triangle, gently push up to receive the needle from the surface.

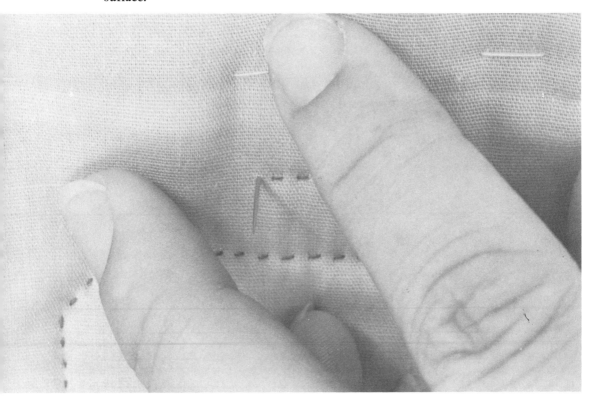

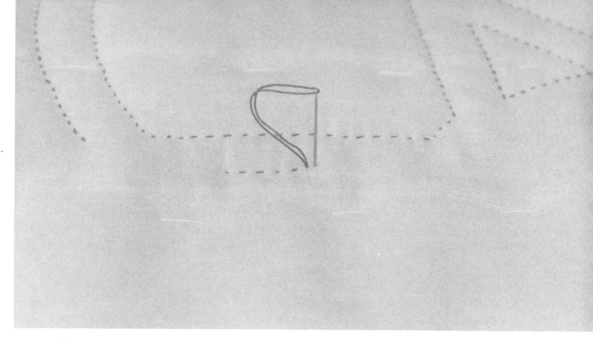

10–8 The needle has been pulled through to the back and turned around to go back to the surface. Again, the needle is going into the fabric absolutely straight. Only enough thread is pulled to the back to allow the needle to be turned around.

10–9 Receive the needle from the back of the quilt and pull the thread taut. The thumb and forefinger hold the needle, but the thread is pulled by the little finger. This prevents the thread from being frayed where it goes through the eye of the needle.

it. Get on with your quilting, and you will develop a callous on the finger that pushes the needle.

If you do quilt with the running stitch, you don't really have a choice. You must use a thimble or risk destroying the finger that pushes the needle through the quilt. Adhesive tape on the finger that feels for the needle tip will help protect it from constant pricking. Of course, you will not be able to feel the needle tip, but you also won't prick your finger.

The "punch and poke" stitch requires very little finger pressure; therefore, you do not need to use a thimble unless you want to. There is also no need to tape your finger.

In Which Direction Do You Quilt?

If you quilt with the running stitch, there are not many options. A right-handed person quilts from right to left or toward the body. A left-handed person quilts from left to right and can also quilt toward the body.

The "punch and poke" stitch has a tremendous advantage in that it allows you to quilt in any direction, regardless of which hand is used above the frame. At first you will find it easier to quilt in only one direction. If you are right-handed, you will quilt from right to left. When you feel comfortable using the "punch and poke" stitch, you can learn to quilt in any direction, something running-stitch quilters usually can't do.

Starting the Quilting Thread

There are two ways to start the quilting thread. The more traditional method is to use a single thread with a knot. The second method, which I prefer, is to use a double thread and no knot.

Most quilters cut a thread 30 to 36 inches long and put a single knot in one end. The needle is inserted into the backing of the quilt at an angle and pulled out the top at the desired location (Fig. 10–10a). The thread is then pulled so that the knot pops through the backing and catches in the batt (Fig. 10–10b).

This method of starting has several disadvantages. When quilting with a thread 30 to 36 inches long, half your time is spent in pulling the thread

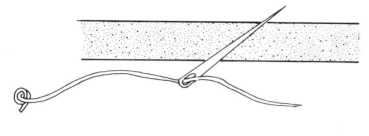

10–10a   The needle enters the basted quilt at an angle from the backing.

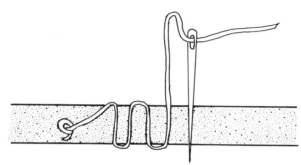

10–10b   The knotted thread has been pulled, with a slight jerk, so that the knot passes through the backing fabric and is buried in the batt.

through the fabric or removing slip knots and tangles. Even worse, the thread begins to fray badly after the first 20 inches have been used, and you end up joining the quilt with thread that may break at any time. You may also have to make several attempts at burying the knot before it catches in the batt, as it tends to pop to the surface very easily. After several washings of the finished quilt, you may also find that some of the knots have popped to the surface, especially if a polyester batt was used.

If you use my method, you'll avoid the problem of knots. Cut a thread 24 inches long and thread the quilting needle so that the thread is doubled. *Note:* You do *not* quilt with a doubled thread. Poke the needle straight into the top of the quilt where you want the first stitch (Fig. 10–11a). Pull the needle through to the backing while holding on to one 12-inch length of thread. Pull the other 12 inches through to the backing (Fig. 10–11b) and then return the needle to the surface of the quilt. You have taken your first stitch. Lay the loose 12 inches of thread out of the way and continue quilting in the desired

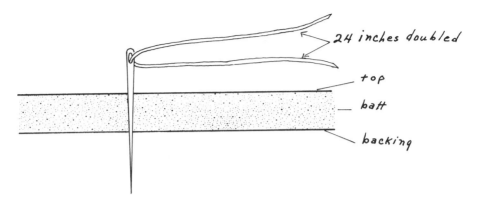

10–11a The needle, threaded with a 24-inch length, goes into the basted quilt at the point you want the first stitch.

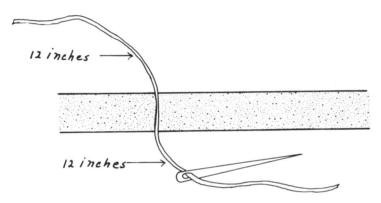

10–11b One 12-inch length of thread is pulled through to the back and the other is laid out of the way, to be quilted in after the first half of the thread has been used.

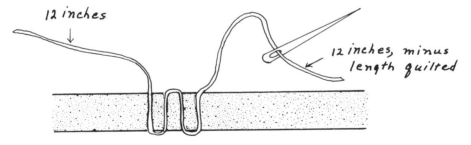

10–11c The first half of the thread is quilted into the basted strip in the opposite direction.

direction (Fig. 10–11c). When there are about 2 inches of thread left on the needle, end by weaving it into the batting. Now pick up the 12 inches of loose thread, thread it into the needle and quilt in the opposite direction. You're actually starting in the middle of the 24-inch length of thread and quilting in two different directions.

What happens if you've quilted a 2-inch square and used only the first half of the thread? Run the threaded needle through the batt to the next quilting line and bring it up at that point (Fig. 10–12). You then continue quilting in the manner just described. Always repeat the first stitch of a shape with your last joining stitch (Fig. 10–13). If this is not done, there will be a skipped stitch on the backing and this will create a bulge.

Ending the Quilting Thread

Always end the thread by weaving it into the batt (Fig. 10–14). Make the last stitch from the top, but instead of going through to the backing, angle the needle into the batt and bring it back up to the surface of the quilt about one inch away (a). Then carefully poke the needle tip into the hole from which the thread emerges and run it into the batt, this time crossing a line of quilting (b). The hole can be enlarged a little if you pull gently on the thread. Repeat this process two more times, always going in a different direction and crossing a quilted line. Finally, bring the thread out the top of the quilt and cut it off flush with the fabric. The thread end will disappear by dropping back into the batt (c). This weaving holds the thread more securely than a knot. *Note:* Under no circumstances are knots to be visible on the top or backing of the quilt.

Holding the Frame

The quilt-as-you-go frame is very easy to handle. You can sit in any comfortable chair or couch. You're not restricted to a straight-backed chair, as you are with a floor frame.

I usually cross my legs and rest the top dowel on my knee so that both hands are free to quilt. The frame can be turned in any direction you desire. If you are new to quilting or right-handed, you will find it easier to quilt from

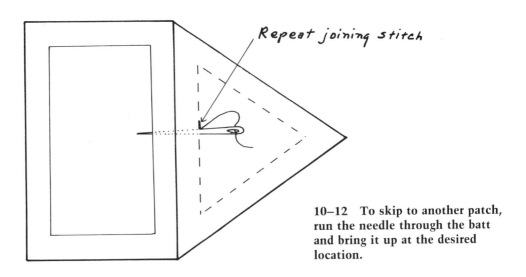

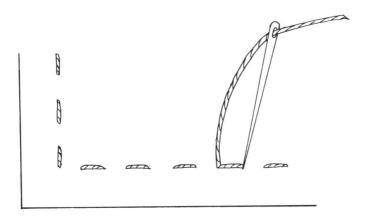

Repeat joining stitch

10–12 To skip to another patch, run the needle through the batt and bring it up at the desired location.

right to left. When you come to a corner, you can rotate the frame so that you are always quilting from right to left.

If you use the running stitch, I'm sure you can see the advantage of the small frame compared to a large, stationary frame—no more difficult areas to reach.

10–13 When ending a quilting line on a shape, repeat the joining stitch or a stitch will be skipped on the backing.

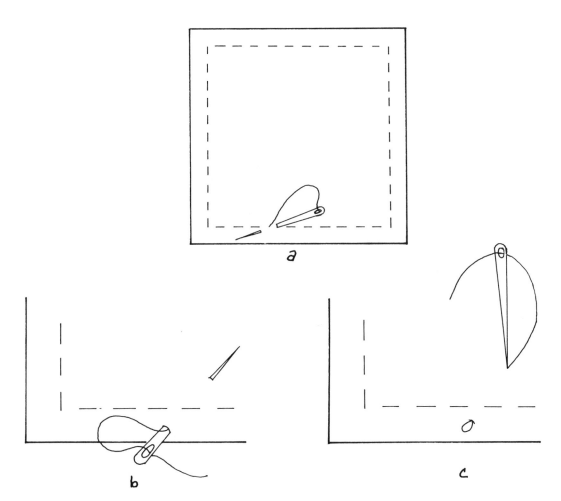

10–14 Weaving the thread end. The needle is inserted at an angle and brought up away from the quilting line (a). The needle tip is then put into the hole where the thread emerges (b) and crosses a line of quilting. Repeat step b and pull the thread taut enough so that it drops into the batting (c) each time.

Quilting at the Strip Edges

The one disadvantage with the quilt-as-you-go method is that you are not able to quilt right up to the seam of the strip while it is still in the frame. If the quilting is brought right up to the seam line, or as close as ¼ inch away it becomes impossible to join the strip seams together (Fig. 10–15). The solution

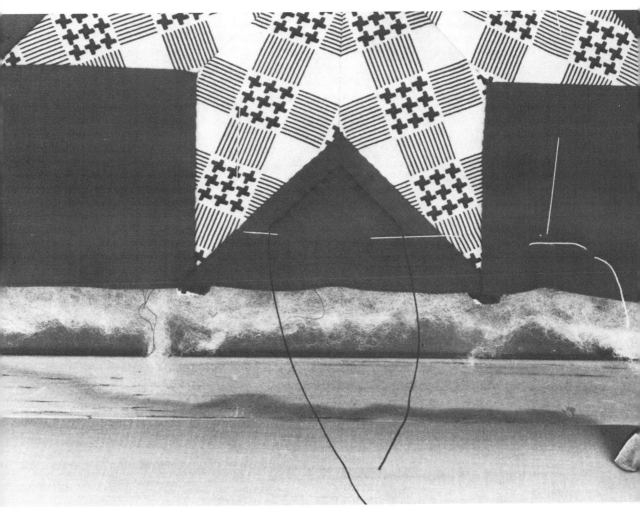

10–15 At the strip's edge
stop quilting ½ inch back
from the edge's stitching
line and let the quilting
threads hang loose. These
threads will be quilted in
after the strips are joined.

186 | Quilt-As-You-Go

is to quilt to within ½ inch from the strip's edge, pull the needle off the thread and let the thread hang. When the quilted strips are joined together, go back and complete the needed quilting. I generally put the quilt in a 14-inch round quilting hoop for this. It helps to keep the fabric under tension, but it's not really necessary.

Quilting at the Strip Ends

As I've already mentioned, the top, at the 12 inches closest to the dowels, will stretch slightly and the backing will wrinkle (Fig. 10–16). This stretched area must be quilted *into* its area. Remember that the basting rows are only 2 inches apart near the strip ends (see Fig. 9–5). If they were 4 inches apart, it would be more difficult to quilt this excess in. Prior to quilting the stretched area, place straight pins crosswise to the "hills" (Fig. 10–17). The pins will compress the excess until you have quilted that section. When the completed quilt is washed, the fabric will return to its normal shape, if it hasn't already done so due to the quilting.

COMPARING THE QUILTING STITCHES

The running stitch is the fastest way to quilt, the most commonly accepted method and, to a new quilter, *may* be the least frustrating. Nevertheless, I feel that the running stitch has more disadvantages than advantages. Unless you use a very thin batt, the stitches frequently do not go through all layers of the quilt, or they may catch only a few of the backing threads. For really good quilting, the stitches and spaces should be the same length on both the top and backing.

When using the running stitch, the quilting needle is held as it would be for regular sewing, i.e., parallel to the fabric; therefore, you don't have to retrain your fingers. However, if you have tried the running stitch, you are aware of the amount of lateral pressure needed to push the needle through the quilt. This is almost impossible for someone with arthritis. You should also be aware of the damage the needle hub can do to your finger. If you use the running stitch, you must also use a thimble.

Admittedly, "punch and poke" quilting has some disadvantages, but since

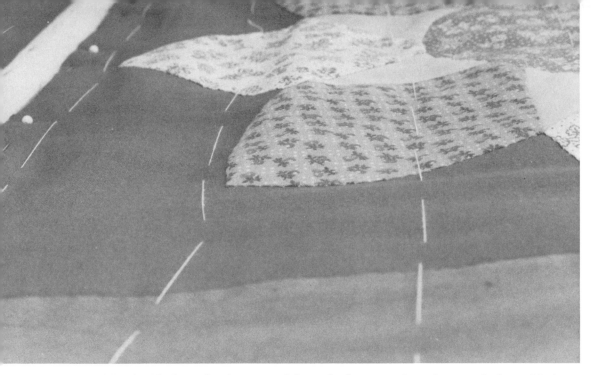

10–16   The basted strip removed from the frame to show the stretched top. Notice the rolling "hills and valleys" between the 2-inch basting rows.

10–17   Straight pins are placed across the "hills" to hold the excess fabric down until that area is quilted.

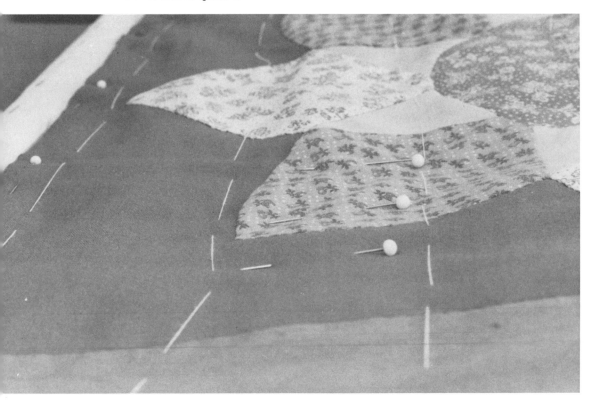

these are mostly involved with the learning process, I feel the results far outweigh the inconveniences. Your major task will be to train the hand underneath the frame to return the needle in the spot where you want it. When I was learning, I found that I practiced for five hours before I was able to hit the quilting line from below with any consistency.

I'm sure that with just a little practice you will be extremely happy with the quilting stitches on the top of the quilt, but the quilting stitches on the backing will be another matter. The stitches usually come out unevenly spaced or on the diagonal. To correct this, train your fingers to hold the needle exactly perpendicular to the backing fabric. This seems to be the key, but it does require time and practice. To check yourself, poke the needle into the back as you would ordinarily, but don't pull the needle through to the top. Turn the frame over and look at the needle. Is it coming out straight (Fig. 10–8), or is it leaning to one side? If your stitches are on the diagonal on the backing, I can almost guarantee that the needle will be at an angle. Again, train your fingers to hold the needle so that it goes in straight.

While learning the "punch and poke," it's a good idea to use a printed fabric for the backing and a quilting thread that blends with it. For example, if the top is red, white and blue, use a red print backing and red quilting thread. The red thread will blend into the backing and not be noticeable. Show your friends the top, and don't point out the diagonal stitches on the back. By the time you are finished with the quilt, you will have mastered the "punch and poke". On your next quilt use a solid color backing with contrasting thread, as I do.

The main thing is to give yourself time. Whether you use the running stitch or the "punch and poke," quilting can not be done overnight. Relax and enjoy it!

Chapter Eleven

Joining and Binding the Quilt

After two strips have been quilted, as detailed in Chapter 10, they can be joined. This is one of the exciting advantages of quilt-as-you-go. You actually get to see a finished portion of the quilt before it is near completion. The following method is used for joining all strips, whether they are strips of blocks, with or without sashing, or a border to the completed interior of the quilt.

JOINING STRIPS

The Quilt Top

Remove the basting rows if you have not already done so. Trim away any loose threads or uneven seams. Place the two strips to be joined, right sides together. Match the long edges. Fold the batt and backing down and out of the way. Pin the quilt top seam on the pencil lines of both strips, just as you did when piecing small patches together (Fig. 11–1). Pin at the beginning corners of the strips and at the intersections of the first block and sash. Pin the interior portions of the block seam line together. Do not attempt to pin from one strip end to the other. Unless you pin in small sections (each block separately), misalignment may occur. Piece this top seam with a running stitch as you did for all previous piecing. Make sure the stitching is on both pencil lines and that the block intersections of both strips are accurately matched. Do not sew down any seam allowances; sew through them at seam-line level as you did in prior piecing (see Chapter 5: Joining Multiple Edges [Flopping]). When the entire seam line has been sewn, press the seam allowances to one side with your finger. Choose whichever side will allow the cloth to lie flat, and be consistent on the entire quilt.

The Batt

The batt is joined next. It is first trimmed and then whipstitched together. Do not allow the batts from the strips to overlap, or the seam allowance area will be thicker than the rest of the quilt. There are two methods of trimming batts. Use whichever you prefer.

I prefer the first method, which is to trim each batt edge so that they overlap ½ inch. Carefully trim one-half of the batt thickness from the bottom

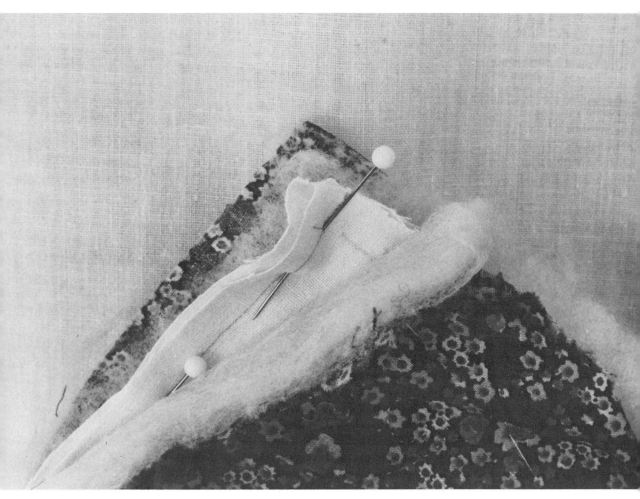

11–1 Place two quilted strips with right sides together. Fold the backing and batting out of the way, and pin on both stitching lines.

of one batt and one-half of the batt thickness from the top of the other batt (Fig. 11–2). By trimming and overlapping, the batt is still only one layer thick; yet it seems to "stick" together better. The second method is to butt the edges. Trim both batts so that the edges just touch (Fig. 11–3).

After trimming, the batt edges must be joined together; otherwise, the batt will pull away from the seam line. Whipstitch the batt, using a single, knotted, white, #50 thread (Fig. 11–4). The stitches should be about ½ inch apart and should go only through the batt. This step eliminates the need to quilt a seam where the strips are joined.

The Quilt Backing

Trim the raw edges of the backing. Make sure that there are no loose fabric threads on the batt. Lay the seam allowance of one strip down flat. Do not fold it under (Fig. 11–5). Lay the adjoining seam allowance on top and fold the raw edge under for ¼ inch (Fig. 11–6). Pin in place. This seam should be directly over the seam on the quilt top (Fig. 11–7). This can be checked by placing your thumb on the pinned backing seam and your index finger on the sewn top seam. If the backing seam is not directly over the top seam, remove the pins and shift the seam allowance until they do match. Pin the entire seam line in this manner.

Using a single, knotted thread of matching color, sew the backing seam line with the same stitch used for applique (Figs. 7–8 and 7–9). The stitches

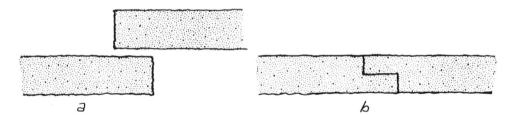

11–2   a: Trim the batt so it overlaps ½ inch. b: Trim one-half of the batt thickness from the top of one batt and one-half the thickness from the bottom of the other batt.

11–3 Trim both batts so that the edges just butt together.

should be a scant ¼ inch apart. If they are any farther apart, the backing seam line will not lie flat. Take care not to stitch into the quilt top, but do try to catch the batt. This way you can be sure that the joined batt will not shift. The entire strip is now joined.

Border Corners

There are two types of corners—lapped and mitered. The lapped corners need no special handling, since they are all straight pieces. It doesn't matter whether you join the top and bottom or the sides first (see Fig. 4–27). In either case, it is straight seam joining as I have just discussed.

Joining mitered corners is not really difficult. Pin and then sew the long quilt top seam first; let the corners hang loose. Start and end the batt whip-stitching and the backing stitching about 2 inches in from where the corner miter begins. This lets you get to the mitered top seam allowance. Pin and sew the mitered top together. Press the seam allowance to one side with your finger. Trim and join the batt, being sure you whip the 2-inch unsewn area. Fold the quilt backing as you did for the straight seam. Pin in place. Check to make sure that the backing seam is over the top seam (see Fig. 11–7). Sew the seam, including the 2-inch unsewn area. When handling a miter, be very careful that the fabric is not pulled out of shape. The intersections of the mitered corners and straight seams should all match and lie flat. Study the corners of Color Figs. 1, 3 and 9.

BINDING THE QUILT

Binding—the last stage. Completion is near! There are a few facts that pertain to all quilt binding, whether you are using separate binding or self-binding. First, binding is the portion of the quilt that wears out first. For this

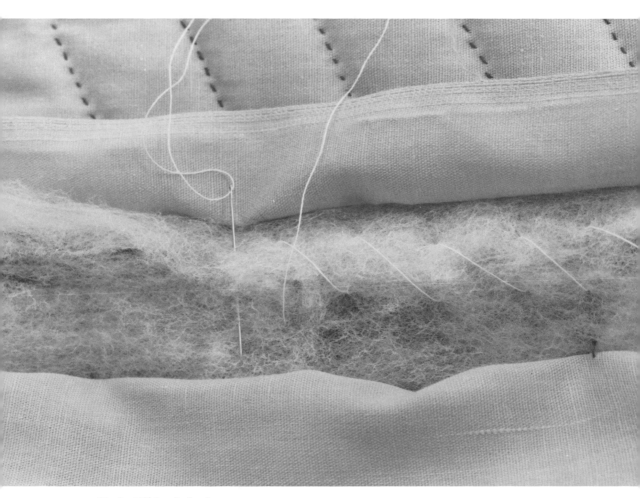

11–4 Whipstitch the
trimmed batt together. This
eliminates having to outline
quilt that seam unless you
want to.

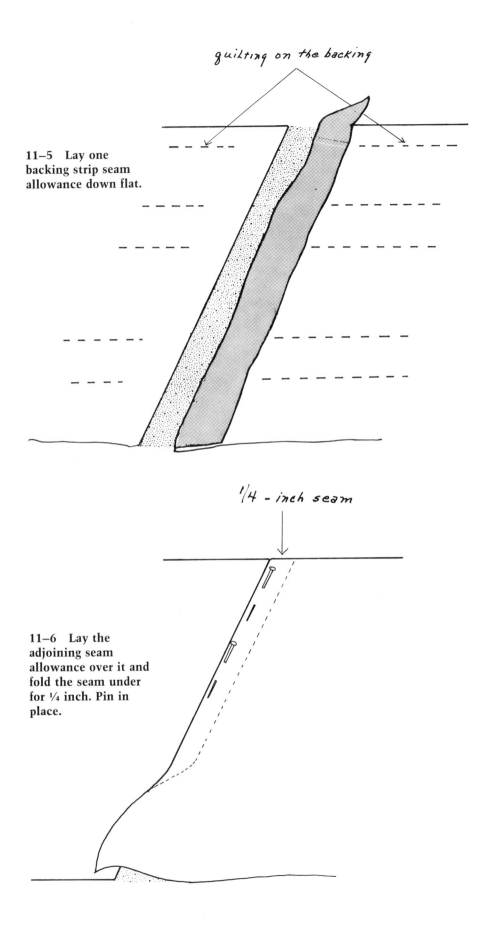

quilting on the backing

11–5 Lay one backing strip seam allowance down flat.

1/4 - inch seam

11–6 Lay the adjoining seam allowance over it and fold the seam under for 1/4 inch. Pin in place.

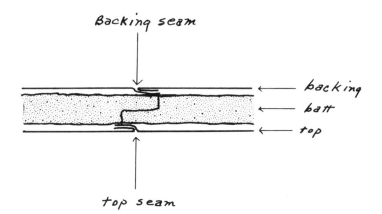

Backing seam

backing

batt

top

top seam

11–7 **The backing seam should be directly over the corresponding top seam.**

reason, I recommend a doubled binding. Second, the binding should be made from the same fabric used in the body of the quilt. Do not use ready-made quilt binding that does not match. Frequently the material is of too light a weave and will not stand up to wear. Purchased binding may save a little time and effort, but after all the work you've already invested, it isn't worth it! Third, not all separate bindings must be cut on the bias, only those for quilts with curved edges. If the quilt edge is straight, the binding can be cut across the 45-inch width of fabric.

Figuring and Cutting Separate Binding

Measure the outer edge of two borders to double-check your original measurements. Multiply this figure by 2 for the outer quilt dimensions. Divide this number by 44 inches (width of material without the selvages). Your answer determines how many 44-inch strips need to be cut. My sampler quilt (Color Fig. 3) is 102 inches square, for a total outside edge of 408 inches. When divided by 44, the answer is 9.2. I need 9.2 strips, but will cut 10 strips instead of just a portion of one.

Next, strip width has to be determined. I like a binding of ½ inch. Bindings should be between ½ to ¾ inches wide on both the front and back of the quilt. A narrower binding will look skimpy, and if it's too wide, it will take on the appearance of a narrow border. Let's assume you want a ½-inch binding, doubled, with ¼-inch seams. It will require a strip 2½ inches wide (Fig. 11–8). The binding will use 10 strips, each 2½ inches wide, for a total fabric length of 25 inches of 45-inch wide material.

Using a yardstick, measure across the 45-inch width and even off the fabric. Mark 10 rows, each 2½ inches wide, including the seam allowances. Cut the rows apart on the marked lines. Hand or machine sew all 10 strips together into one long strip, using ¼-inch joining seams. Press the seams open. The strips can be mitered together, but I don't find it necessary. Press the entire strip in half, with the wrong sides together. It is now ready to bind the quilt.

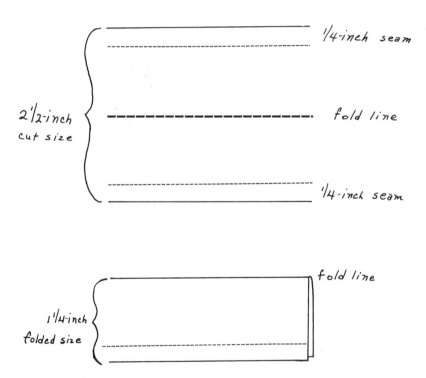

11–8 A ½-inch finished doubled border requires a 2½-inch wide strip.

Controlling the Binding

If you find dealing with all that length of binding very awkward, you might try my solution. I seal a business-size envelope and cut off each end. Then I fold the binding like a fan, carefully insert it into the envelope and put a rubber band around it to hold the binding in place. The binding can then be pulled out of the envelope as needed (Fig. 11–9).

Sewing on Separate Binding

As soon as the first border is joined to the quilt interior, the edge can be bound. This helps to keep the raw edges from fraying—another quilt-as-you-go advantage.

Separate bindings can either be attached to the backing and rolled to the top or sewn to the top and rolled to the backing. I prefer rolling to the top, but again, it is your choice.

Start sewing the binding on about 6 inches away from the corner, if it is mitered; if it's lapped, start right at the corner. Only the corners are handled differently. The straight edge technique is the same. There will be a ¼-inch seam allowance of the binding and quilt border. The batt extends ½ inch to provide lift in the bound area (Fig. 11–10).

Pin the binding to the backing (or top) on the ¼-inch seam stitching line. Using a matching, single knotted thread, sew it to the border with a running stitch (see Fig. 11–10). It is not necessary to go through all layers with each stitch, but do so every 3 or 4 stitches. Continue sewing in this manner for the length of the border (see directions below for corners). Roll the folded edge of the binding ¼ inch over the top of the border. Sew it in place, using the applique stitch (Fig. 11–11). Notice that there have been no raw edges to turn under—at last a simple, fast binding application! Refer ahead to Lapped Corner or Mitered Corner before beginning the application.

Self-Binding

Self-binding means bringing the backing fabric over the quilt's top edge to form a binding. When the backing fabric for the border is cut out, this measurement must be included. It is still possible to have a doubled binding.

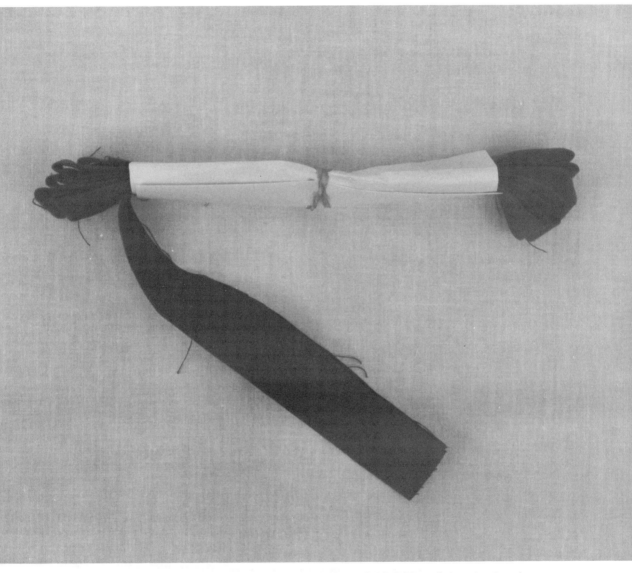

11–9   The binding is cut, joined, pressed in half and folded like a fan. It is placed into a sealed envelope that has had both ends cut off. Wrap a rubber band loosely around the bundle.

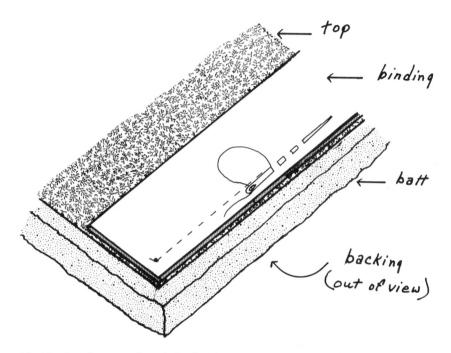

top

← binding

← batt

← backing
(out of view)

11–10 **Set the cut edge of the binding at the edge of the top strip. The batt extends ¼ inch beyond this to provide lift in the finished binding. Pin the binding in place and sew with a running stitch. Make sure that the backing is caught with at least every third or fourth stitch.**

If half the binding is to be on the front, the border must be cut 2 inches wider on that edge and the batt ¼ inch wider to provide the lift needed (Fig. 11–12).

To form the binding, lay the quilt on a table and fold the binding over (wrong sides together) so that there is a ¼-inch seam allowance between the backing and batt (Fig. 11–13). Now bring the folded edge over to the ¼-inch sttitching line (Fig. 11–14). Pin in place and sew down with your applique stitch. Do not stitch all the way through the layers, but just into the batt. No stitches should show on the backing.

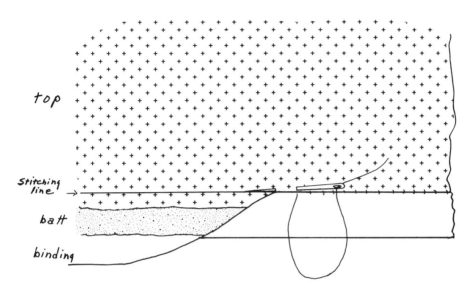

top

Stitching line →

batt

binding

11–11   Roll the binding to the top and sew with the applique stitch.

BINDING CORNERS

The binding corners should be turned in the same direction as the border corners. If the border corners were lapped, the binding must be lapped and in the same direction. If border corners are mitered, miter the binding corners (Fig. 11–15).

Lapped Corners (Separate Binding)

Lapped binding is applied as detailed above, but the application starts right at the corner. The first binding is applied completely from corner to corner. The joining binding is started so that ½ inch of binding extends beyond the corner and is sewn only to the backing with a running stitch. Cut away the excess fabric (Fig. 11–16). Fold in the ½-inch extension over the raw edge (Fig. 11–17). Fold the binding over the top of the quilt, pin and sew (Fig. 11–18).

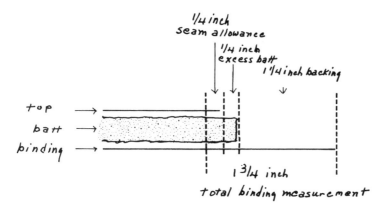

11–12   Determining the additional measurement needed for self-binding when using the backing fabric.

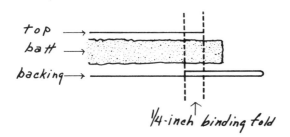

11–13   Double the self-binding so that ¼ inch lays between the backing and batt.

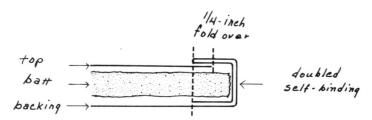

11–14   Roll the folded edge over the quilt's raw edge. Pin in place and sew down with the applique stitch.

204 | Quilt-As-You-Go

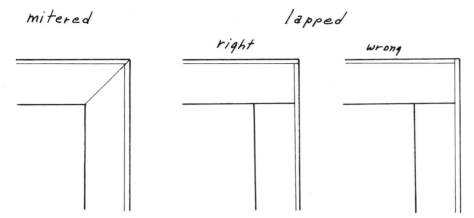

11–15 Turn the binding corners in the same direction as the border.

Make sure this corner fold is closed with close, invisible stitches. Repeat for each corner.

Lapped Corners (Self-binding)

The end product is basically the same for self-binding. Fold and stitch the first binding. Next, fold the adjoining binding over the required depth and cut

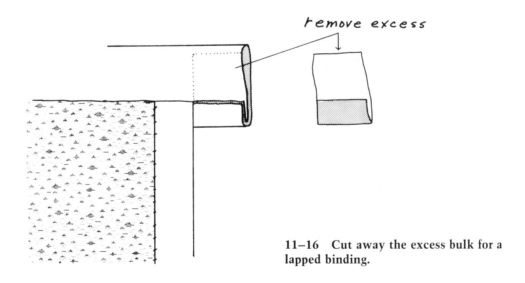

11–16 Cut away the excess bulk for a lapped binding.

11–17   Fold in the first edge of the lapped corner. Pin.

11–18   Make the final fold. Pin and stitch very closely.

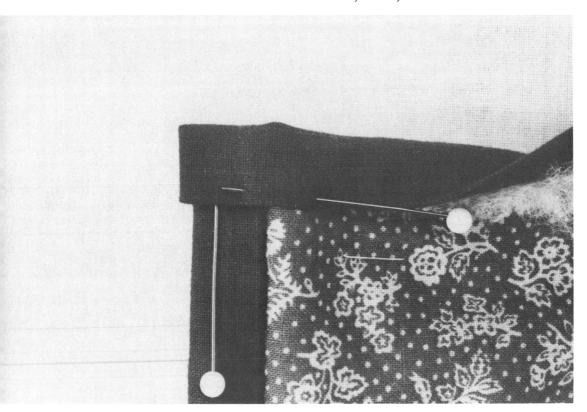

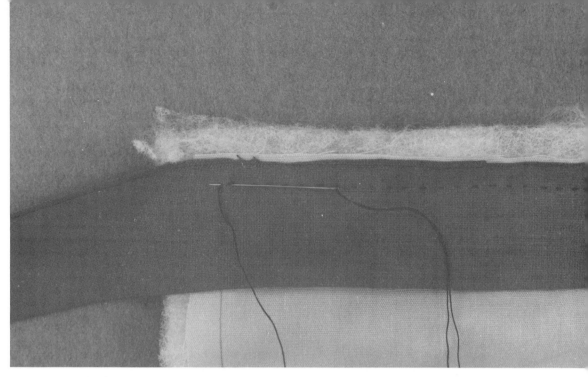

11–19   Sew the first edge of the mitered binding up to the penciled corner (marked on the wrong side of the fabric). Backstitch and knot the thread but *do not* cut it. (The pencil line is shown on the right side of the example for clarity.)

11–20   Fold the binding back on itself. The fold is on the cut edge of the top.

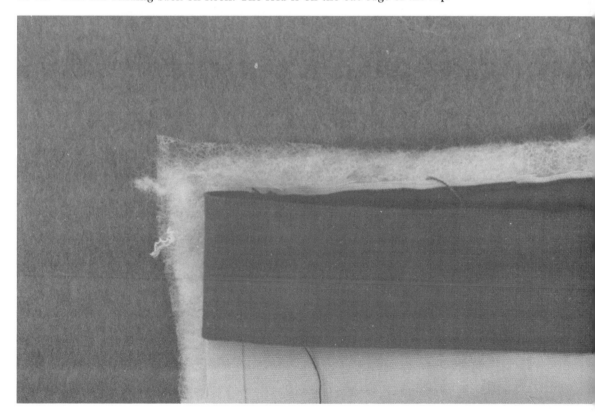

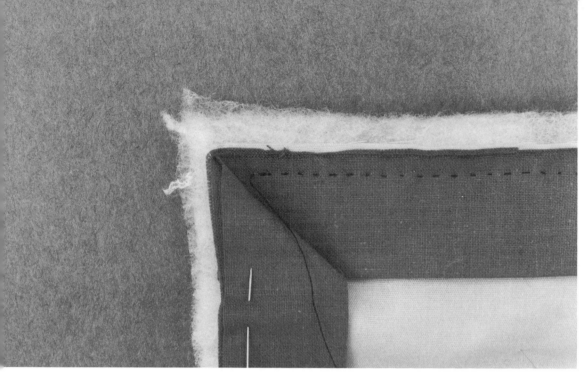

11–21 Now lay the binding along the next edge to be bound so that the binding's stitching line is over the penciled line of the border.

11–22 Hold the binding in place and pull the pleat to the surface.

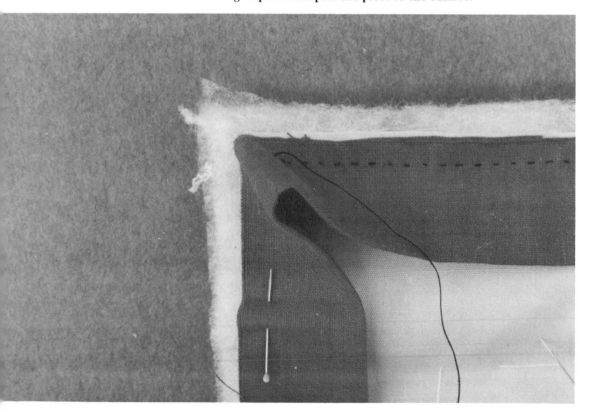

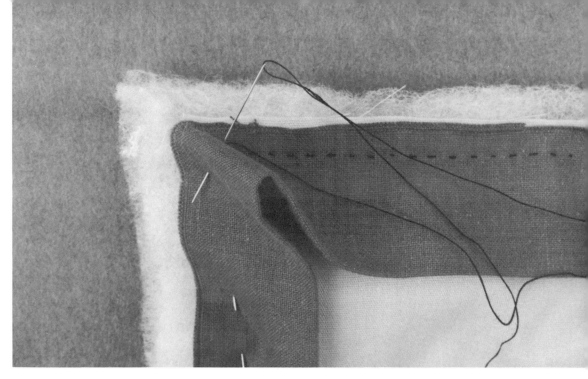

11–23   Stitch through the pleat and backstitch. Continue sewing the binding down the edge.

11–24   When the binding is rolled to the front, a mitered corner will automatically form on the backing.

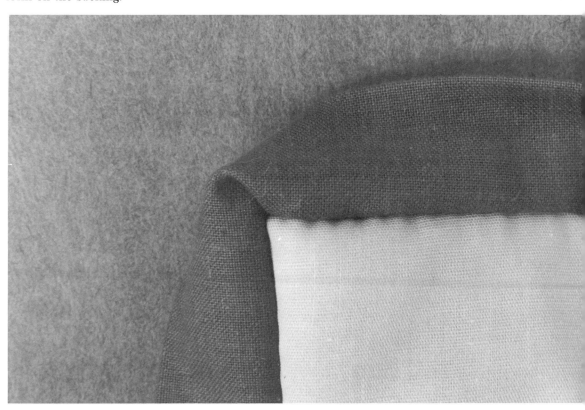

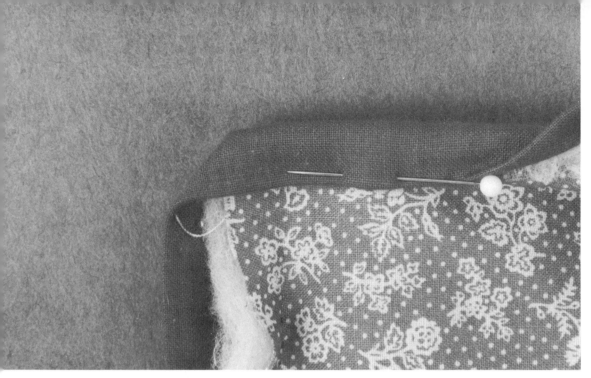

11–25   Fold the first edge of the binding corner and pin it in place.

11–26   Fold the corner over so that the point is on the ½-inch binding seam-line intersection. Pin in place.

11–27 Fold over the binding corners so that an exact, matching miter forms. Pin in place. Sew with invisible stitches.

11–28 A completed binding miter.

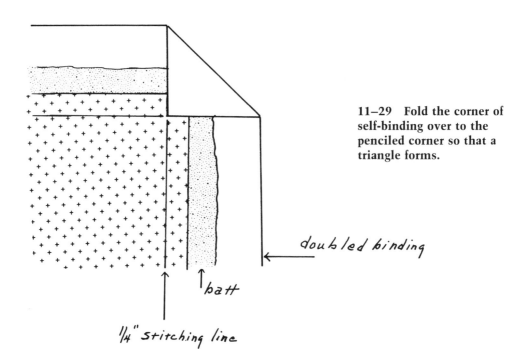

11–29 Fold the corner of self-binding over to the penciled corner so that a triangle forms.

doubled binding

batt

1/4" stitching line

away a ¼-inch rectangle, as detailed in Fig. 11–16. Close the end with small, invisible whipstitches as you continue to sew the binding. Repeat for each corner.

Mitered Corners (Separate Binding)

Mitered corners are never started or ended at a corner (see Sewing on Separate Binding). They are sewn on with one long strip of fabric. Attach the first side of the strip with a running stitch. Do not roll the strip over to the quilt front until the corner has been turned. Sew the binding with a running stitch to where the ¼-inch pencil lines meet on the wrong side of the fabric. Backstitch and knot the thread (Fig. 11–19). Do not cut the binding or thread. Fold the binding directly back on itself so that the fold is on the cut edge of

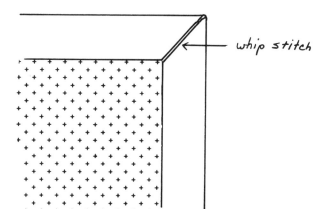

11–30 Fold each edge in to form a perfect miter. Pin in place and sew with applique stitches so that no raw edges or stitches show.

the top (Fig. 11–20). Now lay the binding along the next edge to be bound, on its cut edge (Fig. 11–21). A mitered fold and pleat have been formed. Hold the binding in place and pull the pleat to the surface (Fig. 11–22). Stitch through the pleat at seam-line level and backstitch on that side of the pleat (Fig. 11–23). Continue sewing the binding on with a running stitch. When you have sewn 3 to 4 inches past the corner, go back and roll the binding to the front of the quilt and stitch it down. When the corner is folded over, a miter will automatically form on the backing of the binding (Fig. 11–24). Fold the top of the binding in on one edge and pin (Fig. 11–25). Fold the second edge in so that an exact miter is formed (Fig. 11–26). Whipstitch both top and back binding miters in place as the binding is being sewn down (Fig. 11–27). Repeat for each corner. You've completed a perfect miter in one operation (Fig. 11–28).

Mitered Corners (Self-Binding)

Fold one corner of the binding ¼ inch under the batt and cut away a rectangle of fabric as detailed in Fig. 11–16. Fold under the other binding edge. Fold the corner point down to the ¼-inch binding seam-line intersection so that a triangle forms (Fig. 11–29). Pin in place. Fold over each edge of the binding so that an exact miter forms (Fig. 11–30). Pin in place and sew with invisible stitches as the binding is stitched down. Repeat for each corner.

Chapter Twelve

Drafting Layouts
and Figuring Yardage

In the preceding eleven chapters, I have dealt with the quilting basics. Each separate technique, whether it is simple piecing, involved piecing, applique, strip assembly or quilting, applies to all quilts including the samplers, which you might want to make for a first project. Traditionally made in needlepoint, crewel, embroidery and quilting the sampler is a learning tool that can be referred to for handling a particular problem. Even more important, it can be used as a sample of how *not* to do something. For the seasoned quilter, a sampler showing depth of ability, can also be a record of high accomplishment. It is, however, only one of thousands of quilt possibilities. You may choose, instead, to try a wall hanging or a king-size quilt. The techniques learned in this book will be exactly the same for any project.

This chapter will deal with planning and drafting, whether it is for a quilt or a pillow. When my love affair with quilts began, I discovered that I had to contend with math—my worse subject in school—or face the fact that I would always be sadly short of fabric. I hope you are not a "numbers ninny" as I am, but if you are, I have tried to make the information as simple as possible.

QUILT LAYOUTS

Once you have measured the bed and determined how large your quilt is to be (see Chapter 4), you will need to make a quilt layout. This is a finished drawing of the quilt. It can be a rough sketch or a very detailed drawing with fabric glued to the design (color Fig. 2). Whichever you choose to make, be sure to keep it where it can be found! It is no good if misplaced. I keep mine in a spiral binder with all details noted, including quilt size, fabric samples, amount of fabric purchased, cost of the fabric and the number of patches that have been cut. The last is listed because I may not work on that quilt for some time and I tend to forget how much cutting remains to be done (Fig. 12–1).

Block Arrangement and Size

How do you determine the best way to arrange blocks? It is really a matter of personal preference; no one way is necessarily right. Study color Fig. 14 and Fig. 12–2 for two settings of Crossed Canoes. Both of these quilts have similar colors, but the quilt in color Fig. 14 has a block size of 14 inches with a 3-inch

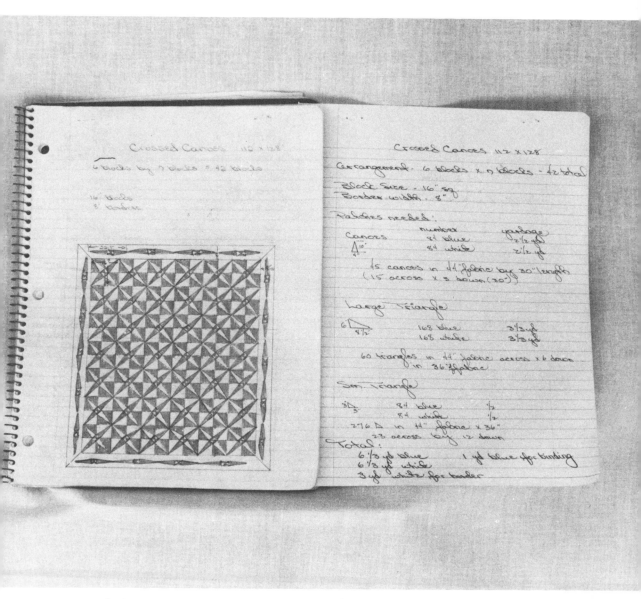

12–1   The layout and yardage notes that I made for my Crossed Canoes quilt.

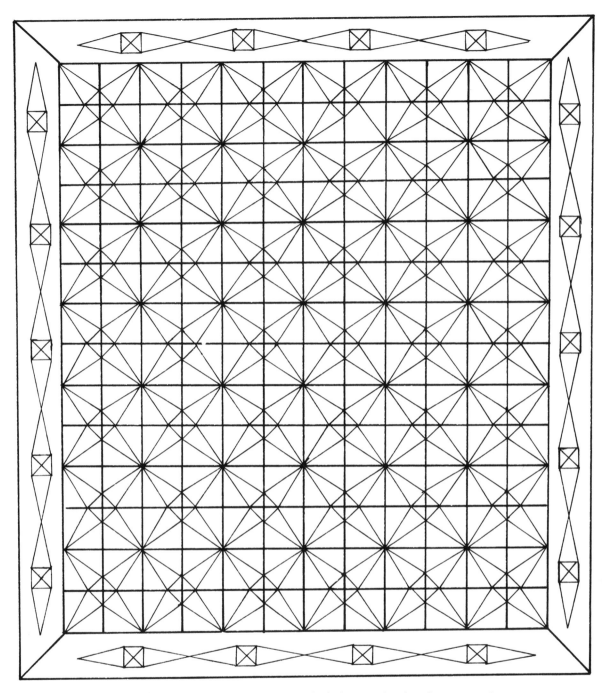

12–2 Crossed Canoes layout. Xerox several of these and color them in to determine color placement.

sash. Fig. 12–2 shows a quilt with a 16-inch block size and block-to-block assembly. Notice how the sashed quilt has a pattern that has been exploded in size, which results in a large, circular, secondary pattern. The block-to-block assembly has a fairly small circle with a star in the center as its secondary pattern.

After you've chosen your block arrangement, you'll need to determine the size of the block. Remember—the smaller the block the smaller the patches and the more blocks needed. I generally use a 14- to 16-inch block, because I don't like to handle tiny patches. If your quilt is to fit a certain bed, this will take some figuring. Answering the following questions will help you plan your quilt.

1. Will the quilt be used with a skirt or will it fall to the floor?
2. What is the block arrangement: sashing, block-to-block or alternate block?
3. Do you want the quilt to tuck under the pillows?
4. Do you want a single, double or triple border? Or maybe no border at all?
5. Will the border be pieced, appliqued or plain? This doesn't affect the size, but will change the amount of fabric needed.

Once these questions are answered, block size can be determined. Block-to-block assembly is the easiest to plan, so we will work with my Crossed Canoes in Fig. 12–2. I wanted a king to the floor with a single border and block-to-block assembly. I needed a total quilt size of 112 by 128 inches. Divide both these numbers by a variety of possible block sizes (12, 13, 14, 15, 16) to see which number best goes into both the width and length measurements. It turns out to be 16. It divides into 112 seven times and into 128 eight times. Since I want a single border, I can divide the 16-inch block size into two and have an 8-inch border. This means there will be one less block in both width and length. My quilt layout will be a 6 by 7 block arrangement with 8-inch borders and a 16-inch block. See Fig. 12–2.

Figuring a quilt layout becomes more complicated with sashing. If I had wanted to use sash, it would have been 4 inches wide and the quilt would have had one less block in both width and length. The quilt would also have been 4 inches longer. Can you tell why? Four sashes, each 4 inches wide, total 16 inches or one block. One block would be removed from the above quilt width, but five sashes would be used between six blocks for a total length increase of 20 inches. The overall length would be increased to 132 inches. This extra 4 inches could be used as pillow tuck (Fig. 12–3).

Inaccurate Blocks

Before dealing with drafting, I want to again stress the importance of pattern accuracy (see Chapter 3: Checking Pattern Accuracy). I have seen any number of students who have been totally defeated by geometric piecing because nothing ever fits. Usually, the culprit is not the stitcher but the pattern. Don't trust any pattern! Remember, a mistake of only ⅛ inch can cause complete disaster. Do take the time to measure your pattern, using the directions given at the beginning of Chapter 3.

What if a friend wants a pattern of yours? Xeroxing can distort a pattern. Don't use a machine with a curved glass plate; it magnifies on the outer edges and not in the center. Be sure you always check your copy against the original. And please remember that photocopying out of books for resale or general distribution is illegal.

Drafting Supplies

No expensive equipment is needed for good drafting, but a few basics are essential. These are available at any art supply or stationery store. Before you buy, check all the measuring supplies against one another. You may find that an inch does not always equal an inch.

Graph paper: 1-inch squares divided into a grid pattern. Grids are available in 4, 6, 8 and 10, which is the easiest to work with.

Gridded ruler: this ruler is divided into ⅛-inch segments and is 2 inches wide and 18 inches long.

Sharp, fine, lead pencil.

Black felt-tip pen with a fine point.

Block Drafting

Make all drawings on graph paper, using a ruler as a straight-edge guide. It is usually not necessary to draft an entire block, but only a portion of it.

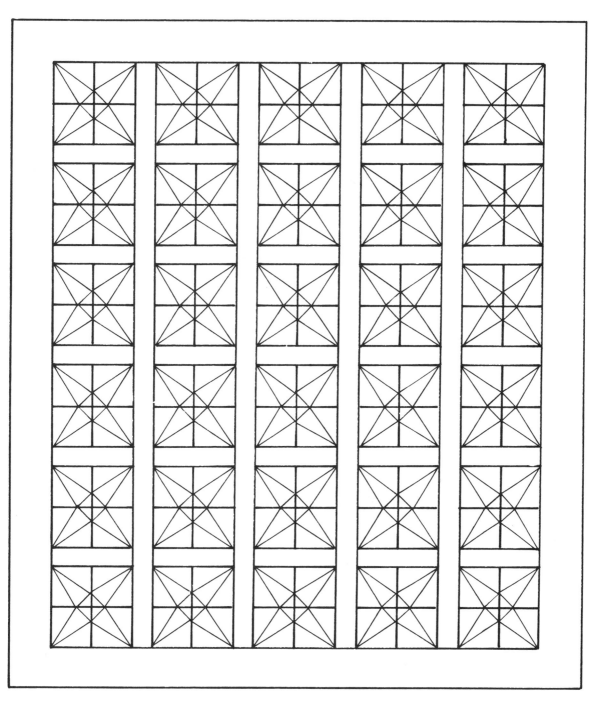

12–3 Crossed Canoes with sashing layout.

Circles generally require full block drafting. Study the block to be drafted to see if it is a four, five, seven, or nine patch.

We will work with the Crossed Canoes block and assume that you have seen a completed quilt but do not have a pattern. This is a four patch and only a quarter of the block needs to be drafted. The block is to be 16 inches square (see Block Arrangement and Size). Make an 8-inch-square on the graph paper by carefully following the grid lines with a ruler. Study the complete block in Figure 12–4. The first line to be drawn will be the base of the long triangle (Canoe). Question: How long should that line be? Answer: Find out by trial and error and decide by what looks good to you. Make a dot 4 inches out from a corner on each of two converging lines and connect them with a straight line (Fig. 12–5a). Next draw a straight line from each of these dots to the opposite corner (Fig. 12–5b). A long triangle has been formed. How does it look (Fig. 12–6)? Not very balanced. Who wants a fat canoe that looks as if it might sink! Try again with a 1½-inch base (Fig. 12–7). This canoe is so thin that no one could fit in it! You will find that a 2½-inch base seems to be the best measurement, and the canoe looks in proportion.

It's much easier if you do have a pattern which gives you the general

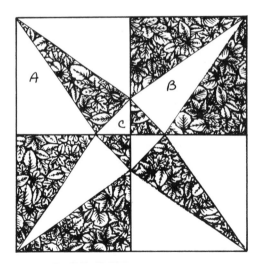

12–4 **Crossed Canoes. It is generally a two-color block, but more colors can be used if so desired.**

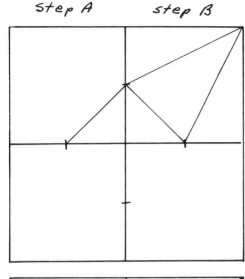

step A   step B

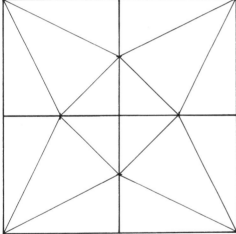

12–5 (a) Make base marks an equal distance from the block center. Connect with a straight line. (b) Connect the base marks to the block's outer corner with straight lines.

12–6 This Crossed Canoes has a 4-inch base and looks too thick and heavy to float!

proportions. You'll only need to "even them up." Use the original templates and lay each piece on the graph paper in the location in which it will be pieced. This is a pattern for Our Village Green (Fig. 12–8). Do some patches overlap or have gaps between them? Make all necessary corrections, using a ruler and pencil on graph paper, and proceed as directed below.

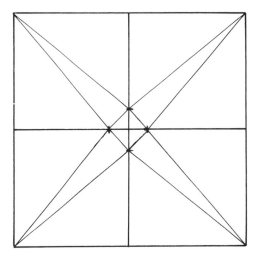

12–7 A Crossed Canoes with a 2-inch base looks as if it were meant for pencil-people!

When your pattern has been carefully drafted, it can be transferred to template material. If Mylar is used, lay it over the drafted pattern and using a ruler as guide, trace the pattern onto the Mylar. Cut out. If the template material is not transparent, make a paper duplicate of the drafted design and cut it apart. Lay each piece on the template material and trace around it. Cut out (see Chapter 3: Making Templates).

Mark each template with the block name and size. I keep my templates together with paper clips and put each block in a separate, labeled envelope. Keep the graphed original just in case you lose the template.

FIGURING YARDAGE

Crossed Canoes is a simple four-patch, two-color design. When it's used in a block-to-block assembly (Fig. 12–2) it's easy to figure yardage amounts. All yardage amounts are determined in the following manner, whether you are figuring yardage for a single block or a large sampler quilt.
Questions to answer (Crossed Canoes layout used as an example [Fig. 12–2]):
1. How many blocks in the quilt? 6 by 7 assembly, 42-block total.

12–8   Checking a pattern of uncertain accuracy. Make paper templates and lay them in a block drawn to the required size. If everything fits, the pattern is accurate. If not, redraft.

2. How many colors in each block? Two. Blue and white.
3. Is the block evenly divided? Yes. The same amounts of blue and white are used.
4. How many different shapes are in the block? Three. A long triangle (canoe), a small right-angle triangle, a large right-angle triangle.
5. How many of each color and shape need to be cut for each block? Blue: 2 long triangles (canoe), 2 small triangles and 4 large triangles (2 cut reversed). White: the same amounts as the blue.
6. How many of each patch are needed for the total quilt? Multiply 42 (number of blocks in the quilt) times each of the answers in Question 5: 42×2 long triangles $= 84$; 42×2 small triangles $= 84$; 42×4 large triangles $= 168$. These amounts will be needed in both blue and white.

Now that the total number of patches is known, yardage must be figured. We will work with 45-inch wide material with the selvages cut off, for a total working width of 44 inches.

First, you must determine how the templates will be placed on the material (see Chapter 3: Template Placement). Then measure the longest and widest points of all templates. In all previous discussions of measurements, I have talked in finished sizes, usually ignoring seam allowances. These ¼-inch seams must now be added to each patch for a total addition of ½ inch; otherwise, you will be grossly short of fabric.

Questions to answer (continued):
7. How many templates of a single shape can be cut out of a single row across the 44-inch material? To get the answer, divide the width of the template (seams included) into 44 inches. Long triangle (4-inch wide): $44 \div 4 = 11$. You can get 11 canoes across. You need a total of 84 canoes. Divide the total number of canoes needed by the number of canoes per row: $84 \div 11 = 7.6$ or 8 rows. The triangle is 10 inches long. The number of rows must be multiplied by the length of the patch: $8 \times 10 = 80$ inches. Since the fabric is purchased by the yard and not the inch, it must be converted: $80 \div 36 = 2.2$ yards. I would buy 2.5 yards of both blue and white for the canoes.

Figure the yardage needed for the two remaining patches to see if you get the answers I have.

Large triangle
Total needed: 168
Size: 6 by 8½ inches
Number in a row: 44 ÷ 6 = 7.3 or 7 patches in a row
Number of rows needed: 168 ÷ 7 = 24 rows needed
Number of rows times patch length: 24 × 8½ = 204 inches
Convert to yards: 204 ÷ 36 = 5.6 yards. Buy 5⅞ yards

Small triangle
Total needed: 84
Size: 3 by 3
Number in a row: 44 ÷ 3 = 14.6 or 14 patches in a row
Number of rows needed: 84 ÷ 14 = 6 rows needed
Number of rows times patch length: 6 × 3 = 18 inches
Convert to yards: 18 ÷ 36 = .5 or ½ yard

Border Yardage

Border yardage is figured in the same manner, except that you work with larger units. First, you must determine in what direction to cut the borders. If the longest border measurement is cut the length of the fabric, it will not need to be pieced. If cut selvage to selvage, there will be seams every 44 inches. See Chapter 4: Cutting Methods, for a detailed explanation and diagrams. My choice is determined by width of border, the amount of leftover fabric that can be used for piecing and the amount of money I have at the time.

The borders are 8½ inches (cut size) and the quilt is 112 by 128 inches. I can cut the four borders down the length of the material (cutting method 1) without having to piece. The combined cut border width totals 34 inches and leaves a 10-inch strip for piecing (Fig. 12–9). Calculate with the longest border: 128.5 ÷ 36 = 3.5 yards for border fabric.

After all of the above very detailed figuring, including the canoes I will applique in the border, it is important to realize that the final figures are only estimates. They do not take into account: mistakes, alterations in color placement, fabric shrinkage during washing. In the final analysis, I know how much I need down to the last inch. And then I buy more! For Crossed Canoes, I

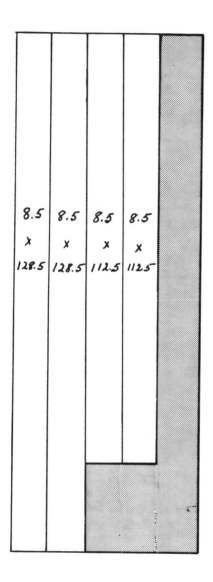

8.5 x 128.5   8.5 x 128.5   8.5 x 112.5   8.5 x 1125

12–9 Cutting method 1 for a Crossed Canoes border that is 8 inches wide.

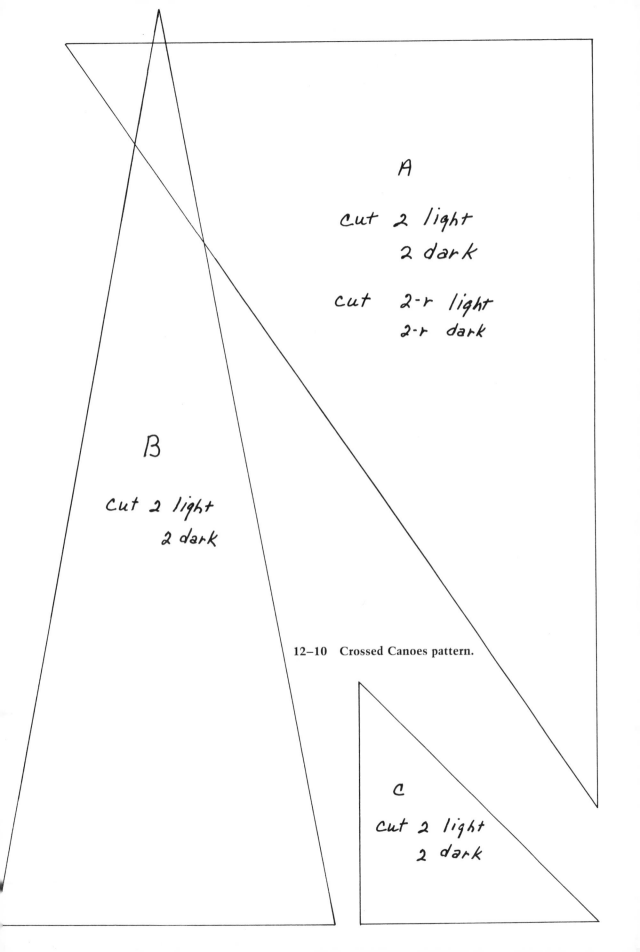

A

cut 2 light
2 dark

cut 2-r light
2-r dark

B

cut 2 light
2 dark

12–10 Crossed Canoes pattern.

C

cut 2 light
2 dark

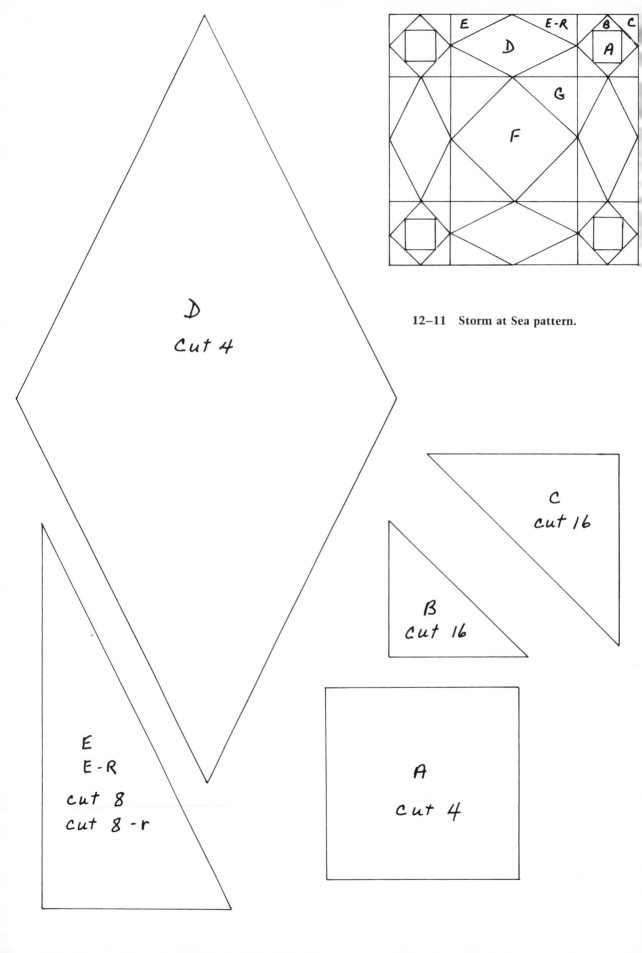

12–11 Storm at Sea pattern.

D
Cut 4

C
cut 16

B
Cut 16

E
E-R
cut 8
cut 8-r

A
cut 4

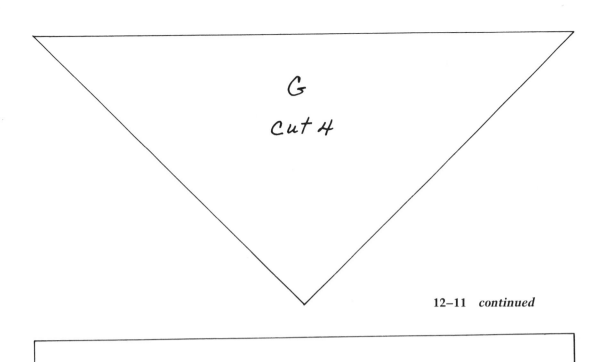

G

Cut 4

12–11   *continued*

F

Cut 1

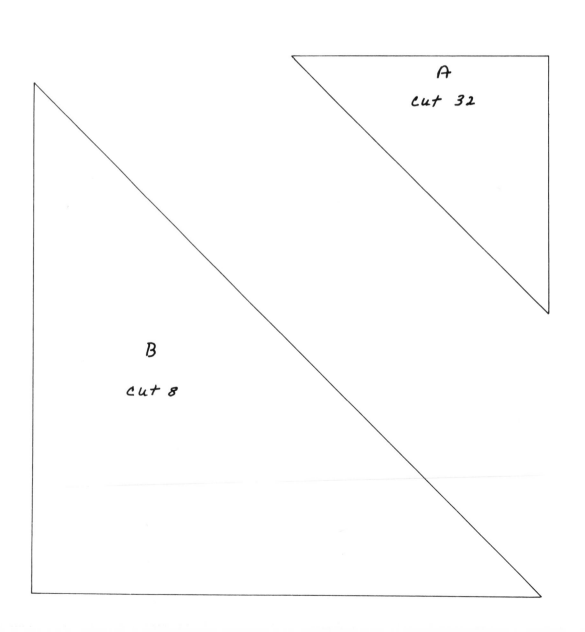

12–12 Corn and Beans pattern.

A

B

A

cut 32

B

cut 8

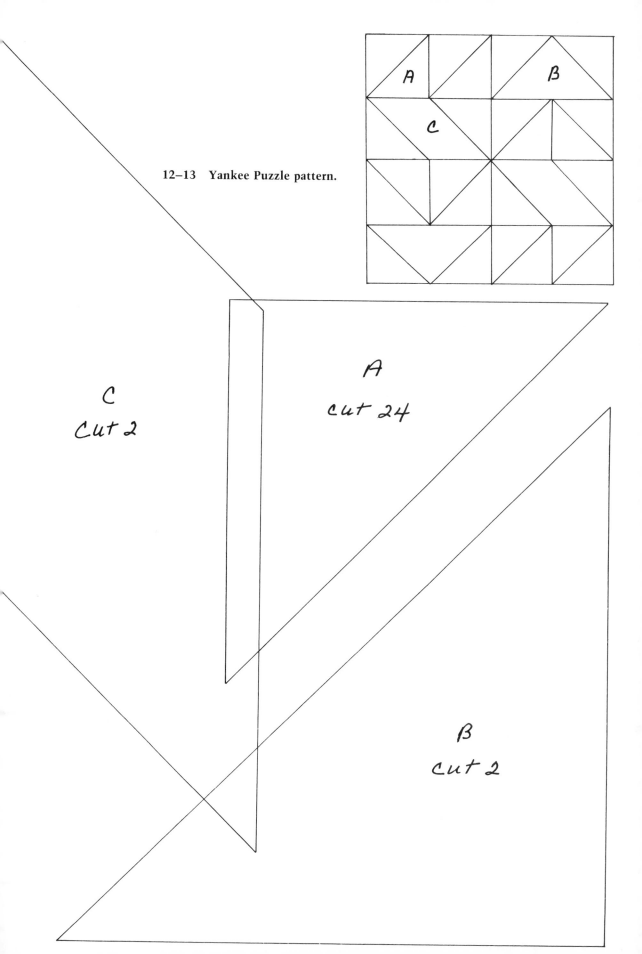

12–13   Yankee Puzzle pattern.

A

B

C

C
Cut 2

A
cut 24

B
cut 2

bought a yard more of both blue and white. It is better to have too much fabric than to discover too late that you've made a mistake.

Do cut borders and background blocks, if any, to begin with. Next, piece one block to see how much fabric is actually used. Do you have enough to finish the remaining blocks? This double-checks the yardage estimates and shows me that I didn't make any math errors.

One additional word about this book: it is not a pattern book, but a detailed instruction manual that will give you the information necessary to design and create your own accurate quilts using a portable quilting frame. I hope that it has given you the desire and confidence to expand your quilting horizons. This is only the beginning. Good luck and may your needle always be blessed with magic!

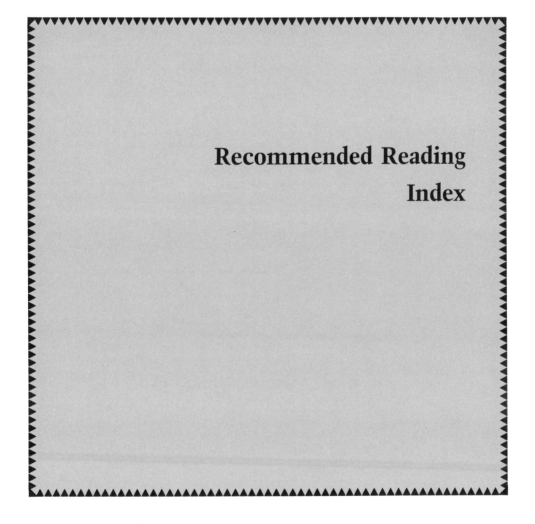

Recommended Reading

Index

Recommended Reading

I consider this list to be a basic library, not an inclusive quilting bibliography. It is broken down into separate topics, but some books could be classified in more than one area. Inclusion does not indicate accuracy of patterns.

BOOKS

History

Bacon, Lenice Ingram. *American Patchwork Quilts.* New York: William Morrow, 1973.

Bishop, Robert. *New Discoveries in American Quilts.* New York: E.P. Dutton, 1975.

Haders, Phyllis. *Sunshine and Shadow: The Amish and Their Quilts.* New York: Universe Books, The Main Street Press, 1976.

Hechtlinger, Adelaide. *American Quilts, Quilting, and Patchwork.* Harrisburg, PA: Stackpole Books, 1974.

Holstein, Jonathan. *The Pieced Quilt: An American Design Tradition.* New York: Galahad Books, 1973.

Safford, Carleton L., and Bishop, Robert. *America's Quilts and Coverlets.* New York: Weathervane Books, 1974.

Classics

Finley, Ruth E. *Old Patchwork Quilts.* Newton Centre, MA: Charles T. Branford, 1929.

Hall, Carrie A., and Kretsinger, Rose G. *The Romance of the Patchwork Quilt in America.* New York: Bonanza Books, 1935.

Ickis, Marguerite. *The Standard Book of Quilt Making and Collecting.* New York: Dover Publications, 1949.

McKim, Ruby. *101 Patchwork Patterns.* New York: Dover Publications, 1932, 1962.

Working Books

Beyer, Jinny. *Patchwork Patterns.* McLean, VA: EPM Publications, 1979.

Beyer, Jinny. *The Quilter's Album of Blocks and Borders.* McLean, VA: EPM Publications, 1980.

Danneman, Barbara. *Step by Step Quiltmaking.* New York: Golden Press, 1975.

Echols, Magrit. *The Quilter's Coloring Book.* New York: Thomas Y. Crowell, 1979.

Frager, Dorothy. *The Quilting Primer.* Radnor, PA: Chilton Book, 1974, 1979.

Gammell, Alice. *Polly Prindle's Book of American Patchwork Quilts.* New York: Grosset & Dunlap, 1976.

James, Michael. *The Quiltmaker's Handbook.* New Jersey: Prentice-Hall, 1978.

Johnson, Mary Elizabeth. *Prize Country Quilts.* Birmingham, AL: Oxmoor House, 1977.

Larsen, Judith LaBelle, and Gull, Carol Waugh. *The Patchwork Quilt Design and Coloring Book.* New York: Butterick, 1977.

Laury, Jean Ray. *Quilts and Coverlets: A Contemporary Approach.* New York: Van Nostrand Reinhold, 1970.

Leone, Diana. *The Sampler Quilt.* Santa Clara, CA: Leone Publications, 1980.

Newman, Thelma R. *Quilting, Patchwork, Applique, and Trapunto.* New York: Crown Publishers, 1974.

Pforr, Effie Chalmers. *Award Winning Quilts.* Birmingham, AL: Oxmoor House, 1974.

Machine Quilting

Fanning, Robbie, and Fanning, Tony. *The Complete Book of Machine Quilting.* Radnor, PA: Chilton Book, 1980.

Johannah, Barbara. *Quick Quilting: Make a Quilt this Weekend.* New York: Drake Publishers, 1976.

Puckett, Marjorie. *String Quilts 'n Things.* Orange, CA: Orange Patchwork Publishers, 1979.

MAGAZINES

Decorating and Craft Ideas. Box C-90, Birmingham, AL 35282.

Needle & Thread. PO Box 10142, Des Moines, IA 50349.

Needlecraft for Today. 4949 Byers, Fort Worth, TX 76107.

Quilt. Harris Publications, 79 Madison Ave., New York, NY 10016.

Quilter's Newsletter. Leman Publications, Box 394, Wheatridge, CO 80033.

Index

Page numbers in **boldface** refer to illustrations

Accuracy of patterns, 24, 25, 220, **222–225**
Achromatic, 20. *See also* Color wheel
Adding patches. *See* Flopping
Alternate block assembly, **44, 46**
  definition of, 7
Analogous colors, 19. *See also* Color wheel
Applique, 96–129. *See also* Master pattern
    theory; Thread
  applique threads, beginning, 105, **106**
  applique threads, ending, 108, **109**
  basting Grandmother's Flower Garden, **80,**
    82
  circles, 119, 122–124, **123, 124**
  curves, 110, **115,** 116
  definition of, 7
  Elizabethan Flower, 122, 127–129, **127,**
    128. *See also* Block(s); specific block
    names
  ending threads
    applique, 108, **109**
    quilting, 183, **184**
  Honey Bee, 86–94. *See also* specific block
    names
  intricate applique, 108, 110–129
    circles, 119, 122–124, **123, 124**
    curves, 110, 115–117, **115, 117**
    points, 107, **107,** 108, 110–114, **111–114**
    stem(s), 116–121, **117, 118, 120, 121**
  master pattern technique, 89–104
    definition of, 8
    drawing a master, 89, 97–101, **98–101,**
      104
    quilting master, 98
    simple, 88, **89, 91,** 92, 94
    using, 98, 100–104, **102–104**
  North Carolina Rose, 108–129, 111–115,
    117, 118, 120, 121, 123
  patterns. *See* specific block names
  points, 108, 110–114, **111–114**
  pressing, 82
  rules for, 104, 105

Applique, *cont'd*
  simple, 87–92, **88–91**
  Star Flower, 142, 148–150. *See also* specific
    block names
  thread length, 105
  traditional, 96, 97
Arranging finished blocks, 156
Assembly of blocks, 85–87, **86, 87**
Attaching strip to frame, 172–174, **173, 174**

Backing
  assembling into a strip, **160**
  cutting into a strip, 157
  definition of, 6
  fabric types, 18
  joining strips, 194, **197, 198**
Basting
  applique, 96
  Grandmother's Flower Garden, **80,** 82
  removing stitches from the strip, 192
  strips, **161,** 170, **174**
  thread, 10, 11, 170
Batt
  butted edges, **195**
  cutting, 157
  definition of, 6
  joining batt in mitered corners, 195
  joining strips, 192–196, **194–196**
  overlapped, trimmed batt, **194**
  seam allowance in binding, 200, **202, 204**
  types of batt, 10
  use, 157, **160,** 161
  whip-stitching seams, **196**
Bear's Paw, 85
Beeswax, 11
Binding, 195, 198–213
  corners, 203, 205–213
    lapped, self, 205, **206**
    lapped, separate, 203, **205, 206**
    mitered, self, **212, 213**
    mitered, separate, 207–212, **207–211**

Binding, *cont'd*
  cutting, 198, **199**
  definition of, 7
  figuring yardage, 198, **199**
  measuring for, **199, 204**
  self-binding, 200, 202, **204**
  separate binding
    controlling, 200, **201**
    sewing on, 200, **202, 203**
Birds In Heaven, 148–153, **149–153,** color Fig.
  3. *See also* Star(s)
  assembly, 153
  closing center holes, **143–145**
  pattern, **151, 152**
  pillow, color Fig. 10
Block(s). *See also* specific block names
  arrangement, 216, 219
  assembly methods, 85–87, **86, 87**
  definition of, 7
  divisions of, **84–86**
  drafting, 220, **222–224**
  inaccurate blocks, 220–222, **225**
  patterns. *See also* specific block names
    Bear's Paw, **85**
    Birds In Heaven, **151, 152**
    Broken Crystals, **146, 147**
    Corn and Beans, **232**
    Crossed Canoes, **229**
    Elizabethan Flower, **127, 128**
    Grandmother's Flower Garden, **81**
    Honey Bee, **90, 91**
    Lemoyne Star, **85**
    Mixed T, **86**
    Monkey Wrench, **85**
    North Carolina Rose, **125, 126**
    Star Flower, **149**
    Starred Circle, **136, 137**
    Storm At Sea, **230, 231**
    Young Man's Fancy, **93**
  setting, 7, 157–159, **158, 159**
  sizes, 216, 219, 220
  yardage requirements, 54
Block-to-block assembly, **218,** 219
Border(s). *See also* Corners
  cutting corners, **62,** 63, 195
  cutting borders, 54, 55
  definition of, 7
  extensions, **62**
  strips, **159**
  templates, **61**
  yardage, **227, 228**

Broken Crystals, 140–142, **146–148**
  assembly, **148**
  closing center hole, **143–145**
  pattern, **146, 147**

Chalk, 28
Checking pattern accuracy, 24, 25, **222–225**
Choosing colors, 19. *See also* Fabric; Color
  wheel
Choosing fabrics, 18
Choosing prints, 20–22, **21**
Circles, 119, 122–124, **123, 124**
Closing center holes, **143–145**
Color wheel, 19, 20, color Fig. 12
  analogous, 19
  complementary, 19
  polychromatic, 19
  template pattern, **20**
  triad, 19
Combining prints, 20–22
  harmonious, pleasing, 20
  print-mixing formula, **21,** 22
Comforter, 6
Complementary colors, 19. *See also* Color
  wheel
Controlling binding, 200, **201**
Corner(s), 60–63. *See also* Binding corners;
  Piecing
  cutting border corners, **62,** 63
  extensions, **62**
  lapped, **60, 61**
  mitered, **60, 62**
  piecing, 67–69, **68, 69**
Crossed Canoes. *See also* Layout
  block-to-block layout, **218**
  cutting method, **59**
  figuring yardage, 59, 224, 226–228, **228,** 234
  pattern, **229**
  quilt, color Fig. 14
  notebook, **217**
  sashed layout, **221**
Curves. *See also* Applique; Piecing
  concave, applique, 110, **115,** 134
  convex, applique, 110, **115,** 116
  piecing, 132–139, **133–135**
Cutting backing, 157, **160,** 161
Cutting batt, 157, **160,** 161
Cutting loose threads, 161, 170
Cutting methods, 54–59, **56–59.** *See also* Layout measurements; Quilt(s)
Cutting patches, 29, 30

Determining quilt size, 32, 33. *See also* Lay-
out(s); Quilt(s)
Diamonds
straight-of-grain, **26, 28**
piecing, **66,** 74
Direction to quilt, 180. *See also* Stitches;
Thread
Double to floor cutting method, **43**
Double to floor layout, **42**
Double with skirt cutting method, **41**
Double with skirt layout, **40**
Doweling, **13–15**
Drafting blocks or patterns, 220, **222–224**
checking inaccuracy, **225**
Drafting supplies, 220
Drawing a master pattern, 97–101, **98–101.**
See also Applique

Elizabethan Flower, 122, 127–129, **127, 128.**
See also Applique; Blocks
pattern, **127, 128**
block and quilt, color Figs. 2, 3, 6
Ending applique threads, 108, **109**
Extensions for strips, **159**

Fabric
color wheel, 19, **20,** color Fig. 12
colors, 19
cutting, 54–59, **56–59,** 157
marking templates, 27
preparation, 22
selection, 18
straight-of-grain, **26,** 27
types, 18
Figuring binding, 195, 198–213. *See also* Binding
Figuring quilt layouts, 216–221, **217, 218,
221.** *See also* Layouts
Figuring quilt sizes, 32, 33
Figuring yardage, 56, 224, 226–228, **228,** 234
Finished quilt sizes, 33
Fitting the quilt to a bed, 33
Five-patch patterns, **85, 86, 93, 94,** color Figs.
3, 5
Flopping, 71, 73–75, **73, 75**
Four-patch patterns, **84, 86, 146, 149, 151,
222,** color Figs. 3, 7, 10, 14
Frame. *See* Quilt-as-you-go frame
Free-form quilting, 156

Grandmother's Flower Garden, 66–82
applique of flower, 105–107, **106, 107**
basting, **80,** 82
diamond, **66, 79, 81,** 82
patch assembly, **66**
pattern, **81**
piecing, 66–74, 66, **68–70, 72, 73**
placement on background block, **81**
block and quilt, color Figs. 1, 2, 3
pressing, 74–79, **77–79**
sewing straight seam, 67–71, **68–70**

Hammer, Doris, Vintage San Joaquin, color
Fig. 9
Hand piecing, 25, 29
Hanger bolt, **13,** 14
Holding the quilt-as-you-go frame, 183
Holes, closing, **143–145**
Honey Bee, 86–94
assembly, **86, 87**
master pattern, **88–91.** *See also* Master pat-
tern theory
Mylar templates, **88**
pattern, **90–91**
block and quilt, color Figs. 2, 3, 4
simple applique, 87, **88,** 92, 94

Inaccurate blocks, 220
Inaccurate patterns, 24, 25, **222–225**
Intricate applique, 108–129. *See also* applique
Iron, 12
Ironing (pressing), 74, **76–79, 82**

Joining batt, 192–198, **193–198**
Joining multiple edges, 71, 73–76, 82, **73–75**
Joining single edges, 66–74, 66, **68–70,** 72
Joining strips, 192–198, **193–198.** *See also*
Strip assembly
basting together, **160, 161,** 170
Joseph's Coat, 86

King to floor cutting method, **51**
King to floor layout, **50**
King with skirt cutting method, **49**
King with skirt layout, **48**
King waterbed cutting method, **53**
King waterbed layout, **52**
Knotting threads, **72.** *See also* Thread

Lapped corners, 60–63, **60, 61,** 203–206. *See also* Binding corners
Lancaster Country Rose quilt, color Fig. 11
Lattice. *See* Sashing
Layout(s), **34–52,** 216. *See also* Quilt(s); specific bed sizes
  block arrangement and size, 216, 219, 220
  Crossed Canoes, 217–229
    block-to-block, **218**
    border cutting method, **228**
    drafting, **222–224**
    figuring yardage, 224, 226–228, **228,** 234
    individual block, **222**
    pattern, **229**
Layout drawings
  Crossed Canoes, block-to-block, **218**
  Crossed Canoes, sashed, **221**
  notebook, **217**
Lemoyne Star, **85**
Lining. *See* Backing

Machine piecing, 25, 29, 30
Making a quilt, steps in, 14, 16
Making a quilt-as-you-go frame, **13–15**
Making templates, 25. *See also* Mylar; Templates
Marking. *See also* Master pattern theory; Quilting
  curves, **133–134**
  definition of, 8
  fabric patches, 27, **28**
  quilting patterns, 156, 157
  templates, 138
  with soap, 28
Marking quilting patterns, 156, 157
Master pattern theory. *See also* Applique
  definition of, 8
  drawing a master, 89, 97–101, **98–101, 104**
  Honey Bee, **88–91**
  quarter designs
    Elizabethan Flower, **127, 128**
    North Carolina Rose, **125, 126**
  simple master pattern, **89–92,** 94
  template(pattern)
    Honey Bee, **88–91**
  using, 98, **102, 103**
Mattress sizes, 32
Miles, Eula, Pink and White quilt, color Fig. 13
Miles, Eula, Vintage San Joaquin quilt, color Fig. 9

Millett, Sandra, Sampler quilt, color Fig. 3
Mitered corners, **60,** 207–213. *See also* Binding
Mixed T, **86**
Monkey Wrench, **85**
Monochromatic color scheme, 20. *See also* Color wheel
Multiple borders, **62, 63.** *See also* specific bed sizes
Multiple edge joining, 71, **73, 74**
Mylar templates, 11, 12, 25, **88,** 156, 224. *See also* Templates

Needle(s)
  applique, 105
  quilting, betweens, 10
  running stitch, piecing, 67–71, **68–70**
  running stitch, quilting, 175, **176**
  sharps, 9, 105, 170
  as a turning tool, 80, **80,** 82, 105, 110, 111–115, **111–115,** 116
Nine-patch, **84, 86, 90,** color Figs. 3, 4
Noon Lily, **86**
North Carolina Rose, 108–129. *See also* Applique; Master pattern theory
  circles, 119, 122–124, **123, 124**
  block and quilt, color Figs. 2, 3, 8, 13
  curves, 110–116, **114–116**
  pattern, **125, 126**
  points, 108, **111–113**
  stems, 116–121, **117, 118, 120, 121**

Outline quilting, 156
  back view, North Carolina Rose, **173**

Patches
  cutting, **28,** 29
  piecing. *See* Piecing
  storing, **29,** 30
Patchwork, definition of, 7
Paper, 10
Pattern accuracy
  checking, 24, 25, **222–225**
Patterns, definition of, 8. *See also* specific block names
  Bear's Paw, **85**
  Birds In Heaven, **151, 152**
  Broken Crystals, **146, 147**
  Corn and Beans, **232**
  Crossed Canoes, **229**
  Elizabethan Flower, **127, 128**

Patterns, *cont'd*
  Grandmother's Flower Garden, **81**
  Honey Bee, **90, 91**
  Joseph's Coat, **86**
  Lemoyne Star, **85**
  Mixed T, **86**
  Monkey Wrench, **85**
  Noon Lily, **86**
  North Carolina Rose, **125, 126**
  Pine Tree, **86**
  Star Flower, **149**
  Starred Circle, **136, 137**
  Storm At Sea, **230, 231**
  Young Man's Fancy, **93**
Pencil lines, 28, 100, **103, 104**
Pencils, 9, 27, 28, 100
Pickell, Joy, Sampler quilt, color Fig. 1
Piecing
  curves, 132–138, **133–137**
    making your own templates, 138
    Starred Circle, 132, **133–137**, 139
  cutting threads, 71, **72**
  definition of, 7
  Grandmother's Flower Garden, 66–82. See
    also specific block name
  hand, 25, 29
  joining multiple edges, 71, **73**, 74
  knotting threads, **72**
  machine, 25, 29, 30
  methods of assembly, **85–87**. See *also* spe-
    cific block names
  sewing through seams, 73–75, **73, 75**
  stars, 138–153. See *also* specific block
    names
    Birds In Heaven, 148–153, **149–153**
    assembly, **153**
    pattern, **151, 152**
    Broken Crystals, 140–148, **140, 141, 143–
      148**
    closing center holes, 142–145, **143–154**
    nontraditional star assembly, **141**
    Star Flower, 142, 148–150, **149, 150**
    traditional star assembly, **140**
Pillow sizes, 32
Pine Tree, **86**
Pinning patches, 67, **68–70**
Plastic templates, 11, 12, 25
Points, 107, 108, 110, **111–114**
Polyester fabric, 18
Positioning templates on fabric, **26**, 27
Preparing fabric, 22

Presser foot width, 29
Pressing, 74, **76–79, 82**
Print-mixing formula, **21**, 22
Printed fabric. See Combining prints
Punch and poke stitch, 175, 177–180, **178,
  179**, 189. See *also* Thread

Queen to floor cutting method, **47**
Queen to floor layout, **46**
Queen with skirt cutting method, **45**
Queen with skirt layout, **44**
Quilt(s). See *also* Quilting
  backing, joining seams, 194, **197, 198**
  basic parts of, 6. See *also* Backing; Batt;
    Top
  border, corner joining, **60, 61, 195, 198**
  cutting methods, 55–59, **57–59**
  definition of, 6
  determining quilt sizes, 32, 33, 219, 220
  finished quilt sizes, 33
  frame. See Quilt-as-you-go frame
  layout drawings, 216–218, **217, 218, 221**
  layout measurements, 34–53
    throw, **34, 35**
    twin to floor, **38, 39, 56–58**
    twin with skirt, **36, 37**
    double to floor, **42, 43**
    double with skirt, **40, 41**
    queen to floor, **46, 47**
    queen with skirt, **44, 45**
    king to floor, **50, 51**
    king with skirt, **48, 49**
    king waterbed, **52, 53**
  patterns, definition of, 8. See *also* specific
    block names
    Bear's Paw, **85**
    Birds In Heaven, **151, 152**
    Broken Crystals, **146, 147**
    Corn and Beans, **232**
    Crossed Canoes, **229**
    Eiizabethan Flower, **127, 128**
    Grandmother's Flower Garden, **81**
    Honey Bee, **90, 91**
    Joseph's Coat, **86**
    Lemoyne Star, **85**
    Mixed T, **86**
    Monkey Wrench, **85**
    Noon Lily, **86**
    North Carolina Rose, **125, 126**
    Pine Tree, **86**
    Star Flower, **149**

Quilt(s), *cont'd*
    Starred Circle, **136, 137**
    Storm At Sea, **230, 231**
    steps in making, 14, 16
    strips, joining, 192–195, **193–195**
Quilt-as-you-go, definition of, 8. *See also*
    Quilt(s)
Quilt-as-you-go frame, definition of, 8. *See*
    also Quilt-as-you-go
    attaching the strip, 172–174, **173, 174**
    directions for making, 13–16, **13, 15**
    holding the frame, 183
    supplies, **13**
    tape, **173**
Quilting. *See also* Quilt(s); Quilt-as-you-go
    definition of, 6
    direction to quilt, 180
    ending quilting thread, 183–185, **184, 185**
    joining quilt stitches, **184**
    patterns, designs, **162–169**
        definition of, 8
        marking, 104, 156, 157
    starting quilting thread, 180–183, **181, 182**
    stitches. *See also* Thread
        comparing the two types, 187, 189
        crooked stitches, 189
        punch and poke stitch, 175, 177–180,
            178, 179, 189
        running stitch, 175, **176**, 180, 187
    strip edges, 185–187, **186**
    strip ends, 187, **188**
    terms used in quilting, 6–8. *See also* spe-
        cific terms
    thread, 10. *See also* Thread
    thread tension, 177

Repeat pattern, **84**
Ruler, 9
Rules for applique, 104, 105
Running stitch, piecing, 67–71, **68–70**
Running stitch, quilting, 175, **176**. *See also*
    Quilting; Thread

Sampler quilt(s)
    author's sampler quilt, color Fig. 3
    definition of, 8, 216
    mockup of author's sampler, color Fig. 2
    Pink and white crib quilt, color Fig. 13
    Sampler quilt by Joy Pickell, color Fig. 1

Sampler quilt(s), *cont'd*
    Wedding Anniversary by Marcelle Wei-
        gandt, color Fig. 8
Sashed layout, **221**
Sashing, strips
    cutting, 54, 55
    definition of, 7
    set-in strips, **159, 160**
    setting to blocks, 7, 157–159, **158, 159**
    templates, 61
Scissors, 11
Seam allowance(s)
    applique, 104, 105
    basting, **80**, 82
    curves, 110, **115**
    direction to press, 74, **76–79**
    hand piecing, 25, 29, 61, 71
    machine piecing, 25, 29, 30
    master pattern applique, 108, 119
    sewing down, 71
    sewing through, 71, **73**, 74
    traditional applique, 96
Setting blocks to sashing, 7, 157–159, **158,**
    159
Seven-patch, **85, 86**
Sewing straight seams, 66–71, **66, 68–70**
Sewing through seam allowances, 71, 73–75,
    73, 75
Simpson, Beth, Crossed Canoes, color Fig. 14
Single-edge joining, 66–71, **66, 68–70**
Soap, for marking, 28
Starred Circle, 132–139, **133–137, 139**
Stars 138–153. *See also* Blocks; Piecing; spe-
    cific block names
    Birds In Heaven, 148–153, **149–153,** color
        Fig. 3
    Broken Crystals, 140–142, **146–148**
    closing center holes, **142–149**
    piecing, 138, **140, 141**
    Star Flower, 142, 148–150, **149, 150,** color
        Fig. 3
Stems, 116–121. *See also* Applique
Steps in making a quilt, 14, 16
Stitches. *See also* Punch and poke; Running
    stitch; Thread
    applique, 105, **106**, 108, **109**
    punch and poke, 175, 177–180, **178, 179,**
        189
    running stitch, piecing, 66–71, **68–70**
    running stitch, quilting, 175, **176**

Storing patches, **29,** 30
Straight-line applique, 105–107, **106, 107**
Straight-of-grain, **26,** 27
Strip assembly. *See also* Backing; Batt; Binding; Quilt-as-you-go
    attaching to frame, 172–175, **173, 174**
    basting together, **160, 161,** 170
    binding, 198–213, **199, 201–213**
    joining strips, 192–198, **193–198**
Strip edges, 185–187, **186**
Strip ends, **187, 188**
Supplies for making a quilt, 8–14. *See also* specific item

Template(s)
    border, 61
    definition of, 11, 12
    making, 11, 12, 25, 224
    marking on fabric, 27, **28**
    marking your own curved templates, 138
    material, 11, 12. *See also* Fabric
    Mylar, 12, **88.** *See also* Mylar templates
    positioning on fabric, **26,** 27
    quilting, 156
    sashing, 61
Thimbles, 177, 180
Thread
    applique thread length, 105
    basting, 10, 11, 170
    beginning applique, 105, 106
    direction to quilt, 180
    ending applique threads, 108, **109**
    pulling thread taut, **179**
    punch and poke thread color, 189
    quilting, 10
    quilting thread length, 181, **182**
    quilting thread tension, 177
    regular sewing thread, #50, 10
    skipping quilting thread to next patch, **184**
    starting quilting thread, 180–183, **181, 182**
    weaving thread ends, **185**
Throw-size layout, **34**
Throw-size cutting method, **35**

Top. *See also* Quilt(s)
    assembled top strips, **159**
    definition, 6
    joining strips, 192
    types, 6
Triad, 19. *See also* Color wheel
Twin to floor cutting method, **39, 57**
Twin to floor layout, **38, 56**
Twin to floor strips, 157, **159, 160**
Twin with skirt cutting method, **37**
Twin with skirt layout, **36**

Vintage San Joaquin by Doris Hammer and Eula Miles, color Fig. 9

Warp, 26, 27
Washing fabric, 22, 27
Water soluble pen, 28
Weaving thread ends, **185**
Weigandt, Marcelle, Wedding Anniversary Quilt, color Fig. 8
Window tracing, 100, **101, 103**
Woof, 26, 27

Yardage calculations, 224–234
Yardage for blocks, 224–227
Yardage for borders, 227–229, **228**
Yardage requirements, **33–54.** *See also* Figuring Yardage; Layout measurements
    throw size, **34, 35**
    twin to floor, **38, 39,** 56–58, **56, 57**
    twin with skirt, **36, 37**
    double to floor, **42, 43**
    double with skirt, **40, 41**
    queen to floor, **46, 47**
    queen with skirt, **44, 45**
    king to floor, **50, 51**
    king with skirt, **48, 49**
    king waterbed, **52, 53**
Young Man's Fancy
    assembly, **87**
    block and quilt, color Figs. 2, 3, 5
    pattern, **93**